HOW TO LOSE EVERYTHING

A MOSTLY TRUE STORY

philipp mattheis

Translated by Kathryn Malczyk

For Sam and all the others

First published in 2013 by Zest Books
35 Stillman Street, Suite 121, San Francisco, CA 94107
www.zestbooks.net
Created and produced by Zest Books, San Francisco, CA

© 2013 by Philipp Mattheis
Translation © 2013 by Kathryn Malczyk

Teen Nonfiction / Biography & Autobiography / General
Library of Congress control number: 2012943315
ISBN: 978-1-936976-40-9

Cover design: Tanya Napier
Interior design: Maija Tollefson

Manufactured in the U.S.A.
DOC 10 9 8 7 6 5 4 3 2 1
4500413876

Every effort has been made to ensure that the information presented is accurate. The publisher disclaims any liability for injuries, losses, untoward results, or any other damages that may result from the use of the information in this book.

Connect with Zest!
zestbooks.net/blog
zestbooks.net/contests
twitter.com/ZestBooks
facebook.com/ZestBook
facebook.com/BookswithaTwist
pinterest.com/ZestBooks

A NOTE TO THE READER

This book is based on a true story, but it is not a true-to-life account of events. When I was fifteen years old, in 1994, my friends and I really did discover a large amount of cash in an abandoned house outside of Munich, near where we all lived. It was a thrilling discovery, of course, but the temptations, euphoria, and paranoia that our discovery engendered also made it, in retrospect, a very difficult year.

Over the course of that spring and summer we indulged our fantasies (such as they were at the time) and attempted to overcome our fears. But this story is also about our more general struggle to figure out who we wanted to be, how we wanted to get there, and how far afield we were willing to stray in the meantime. My friends and I didn't have much of a past, and we didn't have any idea of what the future held in store, but we had money. For that spring and summer, the presence of money in our lives made it seem like the future had dropped into our laps. This is a story about that strange period *in between* events.

For American readers, there are a few things that I should probably clarify. The drinking age in Germany for unaccompanied minors was sixteen at the time, and even though we weren't all sixteen, the overall reaction to teenagers with beer and wine tended to be pretty lax. (Hence our ability to spend many of our days drinking and smoking down by the half-pipe.) Also, our summer vacations didn't begin until August, which is why there are still references to school days well into July.

In an effort to make this story more economical, I have consolidated the various small suburban neighborhoods and towns where my friends and I lived into a single fictional place: "Meining." Similarly, I have changed all of the names here—including my own—and blended certain characteristics in order to maintain a sense of distance and privacy for everyone involved. Dialogues and details have been augmented in cases where my memory was insufficient, and the fates of some of the characters have been altered for poetic reasons. Some minor characters have been added. But in terms of the overall plot and the main events (and transgressions) detailed here, they all really happened. I hope you enjoy my story.

—Philipp Mattheis

I remember the time I found a battered old-time picayune in the road, when I was a boy, and realized that its value was vastly enhanced to me because I had not earned it. I remember the time, ten years later, in Keokuk, that I found a fifty-dollar bill in the street, and that the value of that bill also was vastly enhanced to me by the reflection that I had not earned it. I remember the time in San Francisco, after a further interval of eight years, when I had been out of work and out of money for three months, that I found a ten-cent piece in the crossing at the junction of Commercial and Montgomery Streets, and realized that that dime gave me more joy, because unearned, than a hundred earned dimes could have given me. In my time I have acquired several hundred thousand dollars, but inasmuch as I earned them they have possessed nothing more than their face value to me and so the details and dates of their capture are dim in my memory and in many cases have passed from my memory altogether. On the contrary, how eternally and blazingly vivid in my recollection are those three unearned finds which I have mentioned!

—*Mark Twain*, Autobiography

ZERO

When I saw Sam again, he looked like a penguin.

It was the beginning of April, and it was drizzling. He came up to me and said my name, not quite sure of himself. I was standing there with my friend Will and Will's friend, whom I didn't know. They seemed annoyed by this pudgy, stammering little man.

The whole episode was embarrassing for me—not just running into *him*, but the way it happened, too: in passing, in the dark, after a long day at work. He shifted from one foot to the other and stuttered, just like before. He said he was on the way to his parents' house and that he was living in Munich now. I said that I was living nearby. Both of us knew better than to think this unexpected reunion would change anything. Will and his friend stayed silent.

There were no regrets; no one was to blame. We were each responsible for ourselves, and any responsibility we should have had for each other was excused by how young we were. It's as simple as that.

Of course, I still could have visited him afterward. I mean, Schulz was dead, and Eric was gone. But once my life was finally back to normal, I wanted to leave all of that behind me. I had no idea that Sam would stay inside for so long. At the beginning, I thought he would be released in a week or so. And later—it was almost funny—I didn't even know which institution he was in. And if I had known, what would I have said to him? "Hey Sam, great to see you. How's it going?" Yeah, right.

•♦♠

When I close my eyes, I can still see Sam lying in the sun on the concrete of the half-pipe. He's wearing his beige baggy pants and beige jacket, grinning at Schulz with a slightly idiotic look. He can't manage the simplest skateboard tricks because he never practices, and it makes him so angry that he always winds up hurling his skateboard into the bushes afterward. I see him sitting in the bathtub saying crazy things. I see the four of us hugging, laughing, shouting, throwing handfuls of money into the air. I see some of the best months of my life flashing by.

Now here he was again, standing in front of me. He looked like the Michelin Man, with his now-massive body stuffed into a puffy down jacket. But he still had the same buzz cut and the same habit of poking his tongue into his chipmunk cheeks. (Maybe for the same reason, too, because he had a toothache. One time, he didn't go to the dentist for four years; the office wouldn't let him make an appointment because he hadn't shown up for the last five.) *Stayed stuck,* I thought. *He's stayed stuck.* Years ago, a window opened, and Sam let everything in, both happiness and unhappiness. When it closed a few months later, Sam needed to come to terms with all the baggage. He couldn't do it, and the window stayed shut.

I dug up everything I'd ever learned about the art of small talk, cycled through all the questions you're supposed to ask someone you haven't seen in a long time. I asked where he lived and what he was doing. He asked me if I'd finally gotten my high school diploma. Like back then, it took him three tries to get the word out: "d-d-diploma." I said yes; I had a part-time job now. Sam said he wanted to go back for his diploma, too. I thought that couldn't possibly be true because Sam had never been very bright. Not stupid or anything, but also not capable of getting through trigonometry or writing an essay on Shakespeare with a passing grade. Sam had never been that type.

Will and his friend still said nothing, just smoked their cigarettes and looked alternately from Sam to me, then back at each other. Will's friend had just arrived from Berlin. Will had gone to pick him up from the train station, and I'd happened to run into them. We exchanged a few words, and I'd bummed a cigarette off Will. Then Sam appeared—just appeared after five years. Now all four of us stood together, connected for the length of one cigarette, which was almost finished.

It was Sam who relieved the tension. "I have to g-go now. Bye, Jonathan."

We shook hands, but not like before. Back then we had our own handshake: We used to slide our hands back against each other, then lock our fingers around the other's, and then we'd pull back with a snap. Everyone did it like that back then. Today we just shook hands, like everyone else in the world shakes hands. We clasped, squeezed briefly, and let go. The streetcar arrived and Sam got in.

I didn't ask him for his phone number. Maybe—and I'm ashamed of this now—maybe because I was embarrassed. I didn't want Will and his friend to know the kind of people I used to be friends with. On the other hand, Sam didn't ask for my number either. It would have been an empty gesture anyway because neither of us would have ever called the other.

We didn't have anything more to say; we lived in separate worlds now. I had a job helping people with mental disabilities, and Sam, well, Sam probably still saw someone like me.

There's nothing left that connects us—except this story.

● ● ●

At least, that's what I tell myself.

ONE

After chain-smoking two cigarettes, Sam hopped onto his skateboard. He gave three strong pushes with his left foot and rolled up toward the knee-high concrete block, which had a metal rail on top. But instead of jerking his board sideways into the air just before hitting the block and then sliding lengthwise down the rail, Sam turned his board too soon. He stumbled and fell, his knee coming down hard on the rail. He stood up and cursed before flinging his skateboard against the half-pipe, where it ricocheted back toward him and then lay still.

The obscenities that spewed from his lips had a comedic effect, due to Sam's stutter. It was always worse when he was agitated. In general, his stutter wasn't bad enough to ruin his life. He didn't really get teased, and his speech had gotten better after elementary school. In first grade, when he was the new kid in class, no one understood him, so he said absolutely nothing for a whole year. He was as good as silent for all of second and third grade, too. Eventually he'd had some sort of speech therapy, and then things started to improve. Now he only stumbled over the beginnings of words. It wasn't so bad that people made fun of him or anything, but now and then people would smirk a little. Of course, Sam always managed to notice it, and every so often it would pile up and overwhelm him: He was the only one who went to remedial classes instead of honors, he didn't have a girlfriend like Schulz did, and his parents didn't give him enough money to buy stuff like Stüssy hoodies. "I'm n-n-not s-s-stupid, you know," he would say. Then he would stop talking. Just like in elementary school: He would become mute.

Now Sam shouted: "F-f-fucking s-skateboard!"

Schulz, who'd been observing Sam the whole time, just laughed. When Schulz laughed it sounded like sheet metal clattering on asphalt. As his laughter rattled on, Schulz kept tucking strands of black hair behind his ears. Sam's face turned beet red, and for a minute I thought he was going to give us the silent treatment for the rest of the day. But instead he lit his third cigarette and said to Schulz, "Shut up. You c-c-can't do it either."

"I don't want to do it." His laughter resolved itself into a gleeful grin. "I never did."

Sam looked at me, but I quickly turned away. I didn't want to get involved. Their constant bickering bugged me.

"Yeah, you just lie in bed all day and screw Lena, and when she's not there, you jerk off. Awesome l-l-life, S-Schulz."

Schulz didn't know how to respond. Sam meant it as an insult, but Schulz clearly didn't see anything insulting about it. Plus it was pretty much true. Schulz spent most of his free time in bed—either alone or with his girlfriend. We were all jealous of him. He was the only one who'd ever had a real girlfriend. And not only was she cute, but she was also pretty funny—which was unusual for the girls we knew.

At the beginning of the school year, Lena's English teacher had met with her to do some kind of personality questionnaire. It was his way of getting to know the students. One of the questions was "If you could be any animal, what would you be?" "A koala bear," Lena said. Because her last name began with A, she was the first student, and afterward, she convinced the rest of the class to say "koala bear," too. When all thirty students apparently shared the same dream of being koala bears, the teacher's whole exercise fell apart. I thought that was pretty damn funny.

But Lena was against smoking pot. Or at least she was against Schulz smoking pot. She didn't actually care if the rest of us did it, but Schulz was her boyfriend, and so she had some degree of control over him. Schulz and Lena had been going out for three months, and they'd started having sex about four weeks ago. We knew all about it, since Schulz fed us a steady stream of information about which position they'd used, where they did it (in bed, in the woods, and in the bathtub), and how often. We were sure that Schulz was exaggerating, but even if only 10 percent of his stories were true, he was still a sex machine compared to us.

"You gotta practice more," said Schulz. "The skaters in Munich are out there every day for two, three hours. If you only practice a trick once a week, obviously you won't be able to do it."

"I wanna get out of these suburbs," Sam said, without stuttering. He sat down on the concrete and pulled a soda out of his backpack. He drank some, offered it to Schulz without saying anything, and looked in the other direction, where the train tracks led toward the city. A peace offering. Schulz took the drink and grinned to himself.

"Sure, move away. Just wait till you're eighteen and then you can go to the housing authority and get your name on a waiting list. Yeah, that'll be awesome, when you're living off food stamps in the projects."

"D-d-definitely b-b-better," said Sam, not noticing that Schulz was being sarcastic.

I was staring at the railroad tracks. I kept silent. I didn't want to get involved. Because in a way, both of them were right. There are always two sides to everything (which is incredibly frustrating, because that means that everything is always debatable, or relative, or at least not clear cut). The suburbs with their wide streets, front lawns, identical houses, and the zombies living inside of them, it was all too much. In the movies, something interesting always happens, whether it's an action movie like *Terminator* or just a normal drama. But the suburbs are the opposite of the movies. And because of that, sometimes a good movie feels more like life than reality does . . . if that makes any sense. Anyway, there was nothing going on in our lives. Yet Schulz had a point, since all he really meant was that everything would be better and easier to deal with if Sam and I had girlfriends, too.

• • •

It was about a ten-minute walk from the half-pipe to the train station, and in between you had to cross a sort of meadow—although the term "meadow" might be generous, since it was full of rocks. It was just as accurate to call it a quarry that had some grass. Anyway, all the way from the half-pipe we could see the train coming. We didn't know what time it was exactly, but sometime in the afternoon the train came and spat Eric out. I was nearsighted, but I recognized him from far away because of the way he walked. A month ago he'd been kicked out of school for selling pot to another student in the parking lot. Since then he'd assumed the look of a true rebel. His steps were broad and strong, and he had a certain gravity even when he was walking fast. I didn't know how he did it, exactly, but his walk made him seem really cool.

When he saw Schulz, Sam, and me, he smiled and sped up across the meadow. His eyes narrowed, and he looked at us with the same disparaging gaze that he cast at everything—at teachers, adults, and the suburban gloom. He'd declared war on all of it.

Sam jumped up.

"Sam!" Eric said, and they clasped hands. Eric always said the name of the person as he greeted them. When he shook hands with Schulz, he said "Schulz," and when he shook hands with me, he said "Jonathan." I thought that this habit was sort of ridiculous, but I have to admit that it worked: When Eric said your name, you felt important—even if only for a moment. It even worked on me, even though I knew it was a trick.

Eric sat on the ground and opened his duffel bag. Ever since he'd been expelled, he'd also been kicked out of his house (he'd kept throwing parties without asking permission or even saying anything, and he let the guests use his parents' houseplants as ashtrays), so now he always carried some clothes along with him. He took turns sleeping at different friends' houses. He didn't go to school, and he didn't live at home—he had become the freest person we knew. On the one hand, he could do whatever he wanted; on the other, there was nobody around to support him anymore.

"Dude, do you have anything to smoke?" Sam asked him.

Instead of answering, Eric dug a cantaloupe-sized glass bong out of his duffel.

"You do, I know it. I know you've got some. Come on, say it: You have some."

"Don't be obnoxious," said Schulz. "Let him sit down first. He's got some, okay?"

"F-fuck you, Schulzie. I know he was at Zafko's place. Eric, you were at Zafko's and bought some, right?"

Eric placed the bong on the ground and filled it with water from a plastic bottle. He grinned, looking each of us in the eyes for a few seconds. Then he said quietly but with authority, "Yeah, I got some hash."

"Yesssss!" shouted Sam, tousling Eric's hair.

Eric unfolded a piece of paper on the ground. Then he took a cigarette and went over it once quickly with the tip of his tongue, so that there was a damp strip. He took apart the cigarette lengthwise along the strip and crumbled the tobacco onto the piece of paper. Our eyes followed each of his movements. He pulled a foil-wrapped clump from his pocket.

"How much is that?" asked Sam.

"About a half."

"A half? A half!"

"Half an ounce," murmured Schulz. "That'll last at least a week. If there's four of us . . . or maybe ten days, if . . . oh well, it doesn't matter."

With the foil unwrapped, a pliable brown bud came into view. Eric held the tip of it over the flame of his lighter, and just before it caught fire, he rubbed off small pieces with his thumb and spread them over the tobacco. He ran his fingers a few times through the tobacco, where little brown clumps were sticking. Finally he stuffed the whole thing into the vase-shaped bowl of the bong, lit it up, and inhaled. The smoke bubbled in the water and then rushed into him. After a massive plume of smoke rose from his mouth and floated into the late-afternoon sky, he handed the bong to Sam and leaned back against the concrete wall.

PHILIPP MATTHEIS

Smiling, Schulz pulled his long, stringy hair back behind his ear, bringing his almost triangular face into view.

"Hurry up," he said. Sam could only manage a gurgled "Fuck you" because his mouth was already glued to the opening.

After each of us had had our turn, things got quiet. No one said anything as the sun sank deeper into the sky behind us.

Eric was resting against the wall and staring up into the sky. "Have you guys heard about the house?" he asked.

TWO

It was a Sunday in the middle of May. The air was still chilly inside the concrete half-pipe, but the sun was definitely winning its battle against the persistent cold of winter. The train to Munich thundered by at twenty-minute intervals.

We were hanging out that afternoon—the day our summer really began—because there was nothing better to do. Even if there was, we wanted nothing to do with it.

Eric put on a serious face. It was an expression he'd perfected over the course of the month. I'd been watching him carefully and noticed that he used it whenever he thought he was saying something important or something that had an air of secrecy to it. First he looked each of us in the eye, one after the other (because he knew that would make us even more anxious to hear what he had to say), and then he began: "There's this house on Flower Street." He paused. "This old, fucked-up house. No one lives in it anymore. It's been empty for years. I heard about it yesterday, from this little kid in my neighborhood."

I wanted to say "cool," but something like "ghoul" came out instead. Whenever I smoked, my tongue got heavier than my thoughts and I started mumbling.

"We should go!" said Eric.

Schulz hesitated. "I'm meeting Lena later."

"Lena," Sam countered. "It's always Lena, Lena, Lena. Y-y-you only hang out with her now. Every day."

Schulz didn't say anything. Lena flipped out whenever Schulz was more than fifteen minutes late, and we all knew it. Last week she'd suddenly appeared at the half-pipe and made a big scene because he'd forgotten their date.

"It's not that far from here," Eric said. "If we leave now, we'll be back in an hour."

Eric dumped out the water, wrapped the bong in a plastic bag, and stuffed it in between the clothes in his backpack. Sam finished his soda and tossed it onto the asphalt.

We started off. Sam and I coasted slowly on our skateboards while Schulz and Eric went on foot. Schulz was telling Eric about the day before yesterday, when he and Lena had done it in the woods, and about the mosquito bite he'd gotten on his ass that was now itching like hell.

I knew Flower Street from my newspaper route. It veered off from Main Street and was about a fifteen-minute walk past the train station. It was a little street, only about three hundred yards long. Halfway down, it curved and finally ended in a cul-de-sac, which was unusual because there were no other dead-end streets in the entire town. It was lined on both sides by two-story houses with dark wood facades, remnants of Germany's middle-class aspirations in the sixties and seventies. Not too small and not too big, they were comfortable enough for a small family, each with a garage, a front yard, a backyard, a balcony, and a brown roof. Chest-high hedges and dark green wire-mesh fences separated each lot from the next.

The traffic on Main Street sounded much quieter here when we finally got to the house. I blinked. In the window of a house across the street, I saw an image of what seemed to be a woman ironing. Three times I looked up at her, and three times I saw her head bent over the ironing board.

"Who would have thought," said Eric, pointing back to the house. Its hedges stood twice as high as any of the others. I'd never noticed it before because the house itself looked like all the other perfectly normal single-family houses on the street. Only then did I notice how bedraggled the property was. The windows on the second floor were hung with old-fashioned curtains.

"How do you know it's abandoned?" asked Sam.

"I don't know. That kid from my neighborhood told me. He went inside three days ago. His friend lives on this street, and he said it's been empty for years. Supposedly two sisters used to live here. One of them died in the house."

"And w-w-what if he was lying? Maybe s-s-someone still lives there."

"Doesn't matter," said Schulz, snickering. "We'll just tell them, 'Sorry, wrong house.'"

Eric walked across the paved driveway to the fence gate and pulled at the latch. The gate wouldn't budge.

"L-l-look's like that's it then," said Sam.

Instead of turning around and leaving, Eric went to the left and crawled through a small clearing in the hedge that led around the house. We followed him. The front yard was overgrown, with knee-high grass, dandelions everywhere, and even some old lilac bushes spilling out onto the lawn. Sam tripped over a molehill. Once in the yard, the last distant sounds of the street disappeared. It was completely silent. The hedges hid the view from outside. We were standing in a secret garden.

We went around to the back of the house. On the patio, the seat of a plastic lounge chair was covered in lichen. The glass panel of the patio door was muddy. Wind and rain had overlaid it with a veil of grime. Schulz pressed his face up to the glass.

"What?" whispered Sam.

"Nothing," said Schulz.

"Quiet, qu-qu-quiet!" Sam put a finger on his lips.

"I can't see anything," said Schulz, still loudly.

We continued circling the house and found ourselves at the front door, which was on the side. Eric shook the lock. It didn't budge. He shook harder.

"This doesn't make sense. That little dumbass told me he went inside."

"Maybe he was just bragging," said Schulz.

Eric grunted and picked up a piece of yellowed newspaper from the ground and wrapped it around his hand. He punched through the small pane of glass next to the door. It made a muffled tinkling as it shattered. Eric sucked the blood where a shard had cut his knuckle and reached inside with his other hand.

"The key's in the lock!"

The door creaked open. In the entryway, the air was cool and smelled like mildew. Schulz pulled the collar of his hoodie up over his nose. We were in.

The windowpanes were covered with dirt, and the air was earthy. The hallway was bare except for a layer of dust, which coated the tiled floor, the unfinished walls, and the plywood doors like a fine snow on a January day. There was no furniture. Sam entered a big room on the left, which provided most of the light in the hallway. It was the room with the patio door we'd seen from the backyard. A clothesline hung across the room, on which a faded apron lethargically defied deterioration. Finally Sam whispered, "There's n-n-nothing here. It's totally empty."

Eric paced the length and width of the room as if measuring it. Schulz dug a cigarette out of his pocket and lit it. He shivered. The four of us stood in a circle, took turns smoking the cigarette, and scanned the walls with our eyes. An ax sat in a corner.

When we'd finished smoking, Eric said, "There's nothing in here. Let's keep going."

The other first-floor rooms were equally empty. In the bathroom, the toilet seat was missing and pebbles and debris littered the tiled floor. Behind the bathroom, across from the living room, pipes protruded from the wall, apparently waiting to be connected to something. The walls were unfinished. And that was everything. Why was there no furniture? Why the hell would someone live in an unfinished house? I don't know why, but it seemed almost nightmarish to me—and in those blank rooms I started imagining all kinds of hellish scenarios. It made me think of the movie *Nightmare on Elm Street,* which I'd watched with Eric the year before, when he was still living at home, and we were all still in school together, and Sam . . .

Schulz held a cigarette in front of my face. Sam and Eric wanted one, too. Schulz didn't usually give out cigarettes. When he did, he usually complained about how we were always mooching off him, which wasn't true at all. But this time he didn't say anything, just gave one to each of us.

"This is awesome," said Schulz in a throaty voice. "It'll be our secret."

"It's f-f-fucking c-c-creepy, though," said Sam.

Schulz shrugged his shoulders.

Eric tossed his cigarette on the floor and put it out with his foot. "We haven't been upstairs yet. Maybe there's something up there."

He started up the steps without waiting for us. We followed.

"Quiet!" said Sam under his breath, but it didn't help. The stairs groaned beneath our feet. At the top, we found a plywood door with a padlock. The key was in it.

Eric unlocked the door but it was still stuck for some reason, so he pushed it open with his foot.

Our noses, accustomed to the odor of mildew, now
smelled something different, something more like people:
lavender, coffee, mold, even sweat. The floors were covered
with Persian rugs, the walls with colorful old-fashioned
wallpaper. There was a gray telephone on top of a dresser.
I picked up the receiver; the line was dead.

We went toward the sunlight, which was streaming
in directly above the room with the pipes. We entered a
fully furnished kitchen with an oven and stove, a small
table and chairs, colorful pot holders, an apron, and a
coffee machine with mold growing in it. Everything looked
like someone had left the room abruptly, as if the life of the
room had been frozen at a single moment and been at the
mercy of the elements ever since.

Eric opened one of the cupboards and discovered plates.
He opened more cupboards and found cups, pots, and silver-
ware. There was also an open package of cookies on the table.
Some of the cookies were gone, and mold was growing on
the ones that were left. Next to that was a stack of opened
envelopes that had long ago turned from white to yellow.
Sam picked up the pile and leafed through it, occasionally wiping the dust from his hands on his pants. Then he
stopped. When Eric saw what was sticking out of the letters, he tore them from Sam's hands. Sam took them back,
and then Schulz grabbed for them, and then Sam and I
pulled them away.

"No way!" cried Eric.

He started to laugh, then I started to laugh along
with him, and then we were all laughing. We threw the

stack of envelopes in the air and five blue bills, like old fallen leaves, floated back down through the dust.

It was money. Real money. Five hundred marks.

"Sh-should we take it?" asked Sam.

"What else would we do?" said Eric.

"I j-just mean, m-m-maybe it b-b-belongs to som-som-someone . . ."

"Of course it belongs to someone. They're probably just at the store. They'll be back any minute . . . Yeah, right!" Eric's sarcasm took on an exasperated overtone. "Dude, this house has been empty forever! No one lives here anymore. And if they had any family, they would've come to get it ages ago. This is our money because we found it."

"Y-y-you d-d-don't know that."

"What don't I know?"

"Sam just means," I said, "that we should be careful. Like, what if someone saw us."

Eric didn't answer. Instead, he pressed a bill into each of our hands and kept two for himself.

We left the house; none of us wanted to see the other rooms. We wanted to get out as fast as possible before someone spotted us and called the police.

We hurried through the yard, slipped through the opening in the hedge, and left. As the late-afternoon sun hit us on Flower Street, it was as though we were emerging from some kind of dream world. We ran. We were back in the suburbs—back in reality. But we had a memento from that other place. We had the money.

At the half-pipe we said good-bye to Schulz (who had to hurry off to meet Lena), and then Sam, Eric, and I went to Frank's Pizzeria. Frank's fingers were as fat as sausages—which probably served him well in kneading dough all day. When we arrived, the place was packed with a soccer team, talking and celebrating and drinking pitchers of beer.

We ordered three Cokes and three calzones. When we'd finished, Eric held out a blue bill to Frank.

The hundred-mark bill was absorbed by his fat fingers and then disappeared into the cash register. As he counted out the change, Frank looked up and said, "Grandma come to visit?"

Eric nodded.

THREE

When I woke up, the sky was heavy with clouds. It was damp outside, and I felt like shit. We'd stayed at Frank's until eleven the night before, overdosing on calzones (plus Eric ordered an extra personal pizza; he always ate more than the rest of us) and drinking Coke.

I had a bowl of cornflakes and a cup of coffee, then I left for school. On the way I smoked a cigarette. I never really liked school, though, of course, anyone who says they like school is either a liar or crazy. Today, I felt totally indifferent. Sure, I wished I were back in bed, but I still went to school and, in fact, didn't even really think twice about it.

That was the crazy thing: It didn't bother me either way. I might as well have been sitting in a knitting class or attending a church service. It wouldn't have mattered.

I sat at my desk and felt nothing. In third period I raised my hand to ask to go to the bathroom. (You shouldn't need the teacher's permission to go to the bathroom; in my opinion, it should be a fundamental right.) I locked myself in a stall and studied the hundred-mark bill. I turned it around, rubbed it, and stared for a long time at the serial number, reading it backward and forward, scanning it as if it could tell me something about its previous owner. I made up number combinations, trying to read clues in the random arrangement of numerals. I didn't come up with anything, though one thing was clear. The bill was over-whelmingly *real*.

After school, I went to Schulz's house. His little sister opened the door without a word and then sat back down in front of the TV in the living room.

Schulz was lying in bed. I'd asked him once why he spent so much time in bed. He had laughed and said that he was tired. Schulz was literally always in bed whenever I came over. That's how Schulz was: Even having some-one over wasn't enough reason to get up. He'd ask for a cigarette, wait for it to be handed over, and smoke it, never having moved more than an arm. In between drags he'd take sips from the can of Diet Coke that was always beside him. He said that diet tasted better than regular. (I was pretty sure he drank it because he was worried about getting fat—there's no way that diet tastes better than regular.)

Lately Lena was always in bed with Schulz, and she acted just like him: asking for a cigarette, smoking it, and sipping Diet Coke. At first I had been sort of embarrassed to see them like that. It was too intimate—almost as bad as watching them have sex. I mean, they were in bed; he could have had a hard-on or something. But Lena and Schulz did what they could to make this arrangement seem normal. Now and then I'd find the PlayStation controllers strewn across the comforter (though Lena preferred watching TV). But whenever he and I had been playing too long, and Schulz hadn't paid enough attention to her, she would tell us we were being immature. Older guys wouldn't be interested in stupid video games.

This time was different. Schulz was still in bed, but Lena was sitting on a chair in the corner. The air was thick with smoke—it was as if every high schooler in town had stopped by for a cigarette.

"Hey," said Schulz.

Lena's blonde hair was draped over her left shoulder. She was wearing a low-cut white top, and as she moved to tap her cigarette on a strangely old-fashioned metal ashtray, her black bra strap flashed. Through the fog I thought I saw her green eyes, and I wondered why I hadn't noticed before how green they were, and why I apparently never even thought about eye color. I realized that whenever I thought about Eric, Schulz, Sam, or anyone, I had no idea what color their eyes were.

Then he laughed at me, in his rattling, old-man laugh. "What's up?" he asked. "Money gone to your head already?"

"No," I said. Of course not. I had no idea what to do with so much money, other than order pizzas at Frank's for twenty days straight.

"It stays between us, you know," Schulz said.

I couldn't help glancing at Lena.

"I talked to Eric on the phone a little while ago," he continued. "He definitely wants to go back. He thinks we'll find more. If there were five hundred marks just lying out on the table, there has to be more somewhere else."

"You're such a liar!" said Lena. She jumped up and threw open the door to the balcony, which was near the head of the bed.

"Come out here," she said. She didn't mean Schulz, she meant me.

I threw Schulz a questioning glance, but he just stared at a point in the distance, beyond the white wall of his room. Lena and I didn't know each other that well, but sometimes I had the impression that she wanted me to be her ally. She seemed to think I was likely to take her side in an argument or talk to her when she got worked up—which should have been Schulz's job, not mine.

Lena leaned over the wooden rail and looked out past the fields and toward the woods. The pine trees were dark green, as always (which is why, in my opinion, pine trees are so boring). I tried hard not to look at Lena's ass, which, with her back stretched out, looked even more amazing than usual.

When she'd smoked half her cigarette, she said, "He hasn't talked about anything else since yesterday. It's all about this money. He wants to buy a car—and he doesn't even have his license. He says that next time you're going to find a thousand. You guys stole that money! Right? I mean, it has to belong to someone!"

"Well, but the door was already open . . ."

"He said you kicked it in."

"No, he's exaggerating," I assured her. "It was already open. For sure."

"It doesn't matter. I still don't want you going back in. It's just gonna cause problems."

She threw her cigarette down into the garden below—which always made Schulz's mom incredibly upset—and went back in.

"I gotta go," she said, and slipped on a black wool jacket. "I've got a French test coming up."

When she'd left the room, Schulz got up. He was wearing a T-shirt and multicolored boxers that were too wide for his skinny legs. He looked like a rooster poking around the farmyard.

"She should be happy. But instead, she just gets all self-righteous about it. Even though she's the one who cheats," he said, pulling his pants on.

"She's cheating on you?"

"No, not on me. But she started hooking up with me while she was still with her ex. I shouldn't really care, but sometimes I feel kinda sorry for him. I mean, I can understand: It's me." He grinned. "But who knows what'll happen when she meets someone hotter than me, you know?"

"Whatever."

"Yeah, whatever, it doesn't matter. Let's grab some beer at the gas station and get out of here."

"Beer?" I asked. We hadn't been drinking much lately. Eric's hash supply had been the focus of our attention instead.

"Yeah, remember beer? That used to be fun. Let's go."

There are two places you can always count on: gas stations and McDonald's, little lighthouses where everything is always the same. A strawberry-blonde girl about our age was working the register, asking the man at the counter, "These two?" The scanner chirped. We each grabbed four beers from the fridge.

"Forty-three eighty-nine," the girl was saying.

Schulz got a bag of chips. I went to the magazine rack.

"And six eleven is your change. Thank you."

Schulz got two Snickers off the shelf. I stuck a *Playboy* under my arm. He got two minibottles of Smirnoff. "Get four," I said, and he got eight.

"And a pack of Marlboro Mediums," Schulz said to the girl when we reached the counter.

"A pack of Marlboro Mediums," she repeated.

"And a pack of Winstons," I added. I suddenly had an overpowering urge to laugh.

"Blue or red?"

"Uh, the . . ." I couldn't hold the laughter back anymore. I snorted.

"Sorry?"

"He wants red," Schulz said, helping me, but he was laughing, too.

"Have you been smoking pot?" asked the girl.

Tears filled my eyes as I pulled myself together. "Uh, no, we were just . . . uh . . ."

"Thirty-nine fifty-six, please."

I pulled the blue bill from my pocket and gave it to her. She gave me my change. We stowed everything in our backpacks, and as we walked out the door, I heard her say, "Bye."

We sat down inside the little bus shelter near the half-pipe, the one place it was dry. And for the first time in a long time, Schulz didn't talk about sex. "We're so lucky," he said. "I mean, it can't get much better than this, right? To us."

Making a toast "to us" would normally be a pretty lame thing to do, especially when it's one guy saying it to another—but at that moment I thought it was perfect. He was right: The money really was a huge stroke of luck. Not just because now we could afford stuff like Smirnoff and beer, but also because something had finally happened to us.

We each took a drink of beer, but since I wasn't used to it anymore, I choked and coughed a bit on the foam. Then we toasted again with our mini-Smirnoffs and chugged them.

"Tomorrow we'll go back in," said Schulz.

FOUR

Eric sat Indian-style on his sleeping bag, his head bent over a piece of paper. He was rubbing little pieces off a brown bud. He'd pulled his hood over his face so that you could only see his thick red goatee. The bud had dwindled away over the last two days and now only half of it was left. It was still drizzling, and Eric smelled like a wet dog that had been dipped in cologne. "Davidoff. Smells pretty good, huh?"

"H-has it really been two days since you took a shower? Since Lydia's parents kicked you out of their house?" asked Sam.

He shook his head. "It's not important to me right now," he said. "Anyway, it's bad for your skin if you shower too much."

As it turned out, Eric had spent the night at the half-pipe. For the past two weeks, he'd stayed at the house of his sort-of-girlfriend Lydia, but her parents had had enough of him. In two days he could go to his friend Daniel's, since Daniel's parents would be gone for three weeks. Until then, Eric said he was going to "just sleep outside."

"You're crazy," Schulz said, but Eric just shrugged.

The water bubbled as Eric sucked on the bong. The sky was still overcast and a mild wind was blowing down from the mountains.

The asphalt was wet, and since water was bad for the coating on our skateboards, we decided to walk. Sam wore his beat-up Yankees cap and the rest of us had our hoodies pulled over our heads.

We turned onto Flower Street. The closer we got to the house, the quieter it got. Just before we got to the house, I looked across the street and flinched: There she was again, the same ghostly figure, standing behind the window and ironing.

"Just like my mom," Schulz said. "She irons every day." I realized that the woman wasn't just in my imagination after all.

"Shouldn't we make sure that no one sees us?" asked Sam. "I mean, the afternoon is n-n-not exactly the best time to be going into a s-s-stranger's house."

"Fuck that," said Eric. "Except for that lady ironing upstairs, there's no one around. And if we came poking around here at night with flashlights, that would be even more suspicious."

I'd brought a flashlight and a pocketknife. I wasn't sure exactly what I was going to do with them, but having them made me feel like MacGyver.

The wind blew through the hedges and shook them. The air smelled like herbs. Eric was the first one over the fence gate again, and we followed after him, disappearing behind the hedge.

The grass was wet and soaked through my shoes. Flower buds and bits of hedge stuck to my ankles. Schulz ran up to the patio and pressed his face against the streaky glass. We turned around the third corner and were almost to the front door when we heard Schulz shout: "Wait! This one's open!"

We ran back. Schulz pushed against the glass door and it opened effortlessly. We followed behind and found ourselves once again in the empty, dusty room with the clothesline. Apparently, we'd broken the windowpane for nothing.

Eric said, "So that kid from my neighborhood wasn't lying. He must have come in through the patio door. We were just too stupid to try it."

"Or someone else opened the door after we were inside," murmured Schulz. He'd pulled the collar of his hoodie up over his nose so that only his eyes were visible.

"There's no way," said Eric. "Who else would've come here?"

We went through the rooms on the first floor, as if to check whether anything had changed since our last visit. But everything was just like we remembered: The whole first floor was unfinished. Maybe the owner had started a renovation and never completed it, or maybe it had always been like this. It was like a skeleton.

I remembered the little flashlight I'd brought from home, and I suggested we check out the basement.

Our shoes crunched over pebbles as we descended the basement stairs. We inhaled the cold, stale air. Behind his improvised face mask, Schulz whistled the *Sesame Street* song, which sounded really ridiculous. Sam gave him a shove, and Schulz looked like he wanted to shove him back, but by then we were all standing at the bottom, and there was no more time for messing around. Nervously, I swept the flashlight beam along the walls. They were bare concrete. A small streak of daylight came in from a window well, but we still needed the flashlight. I moved farther into the room when Sam suddenly shouted. I jumped. In the middle of the room was a mound, a knee-high pile of rocks, soil, and bits of concrete. It was an oblong shape, about six feet long. Next to it, a shovel leaned against the wall.

"Sh-sh-shit, someone's b-b-buried here! They buried someone! They killed someone! A dead body! This is a g-g-grave. Look, it's a grave, it's shaped like a coffin!"

"Chill out, Sam," said Eric, and he took the flashlight from my hand.

"I w-w-wanna g-g-get out of here." Sam headed for the steps.

Schulz whistled louder and even more obnoxiously. Nothing could have been less appropriate than whistling "Sunny Day / Sweepin' the clouds away / on my way to

where the air is sweet." Just as I was about to say "Schulz!"
Eric grabbed Sam's shoulder.

"It's just a pile of rocks. There's no dead body. It's
just rocks and gravel. Got it?"

He took the shovel and poked around in the pile.
He tossed three or four large shovelfuls into the corner to
prove nothing was under the rocks except more rocks.

Eric pointed the flashlight over the ground, but there
was no floor, or at least not a real one. The whole basement was just a layer of gravel.

"They didn't even put in a floor," said Eric.

In the meantime, Sam had lit a cigarette, which he
was smoking with a shaky hand. He kept murmuring
"g-g-ghosts, ghosts," and glancing alternately left and
right. He looked almost disoriented.

Schulz was still whistling. "Can you tell me how to
get / how to get to Sesame Street."

"I've had enough of this. Let's go back up," said Eric.

Quickly, but still slowly enough that we wouldn't
trip, we teetered up the steps into daylight. In contrast to
the basement, the first floor now seemed almost cozy. Sam
had gotten up his courage again. Or at least enough to give
Schulz a sharp kick in the shin.

"Stop it with the fucking *Sesame Street* song!"

Schulz gave a muffled "ow" through his face mask
and finally stopped whistling.

"Why the hell is there no floor? Who builds a house
without a floor?" I asked.

Schulz laughed nervously.

"D-d-dumbass," said Sam. He took off his hat and rubbed his close-cropped hair. "Maybe there really was a body downstairs."

"I doubt it," said Eric. "It's just a construction site. You watch too many horror movies."

"Why d-d-don't we toke up here?" Sam asked.

"Because you just flipped your shit," said Schulz.

"Y-y-you're scared shitless and whistling *Sesame Street* the whole time!"

While Schulz was deciding what to say, Eric had already unpacked the bong. We were going to do it: We were going to smoke up in this spooky old house.

I liked the way the musty air mingled with the sweet-smelling weed. It was as if someone had stopped time inside this house, and now time was starting up again because we were doing something no one had ever done in here before.

Afterward, we went up the stairs to the second floor. But instead of sticking together timidly, like last time, we each went our own way. Sam ran into the room at the end of the hallway and I followed him. It was a living room with a piano and a dusty green velvet couch. Oil paintings of hunters and deer hung from walls covered in patterned beige wallpaper. Schulz shouted loudly from another room, but I couldn't make out what he was saying. I went to find him as Sam was opening cabinets full of dishes.

Schulz was standing in a small bedroom, one story above the patio and two stories above the grimy basement. He'd pulled the mattress off the bed, and dust particles were swirling through the air. A pile of envelopes appeared, shaded yellow and sprinkled gray with time.

Schulz let the mattress fall with a jerk. We hurriedly opened envelope after envelope. In the meantime Eric was inspecting the flooring around the second floor. When Schulz and I went out into the hallway, envelopes in hand, he was kneeling at the end of a long reddish Persian rug and trying to roll it up. Underneath was light gray linoleum, offering a glimpse into the past, back when this house was brand new. Eric, rolling chaotically, kept tangling up the rug and having to start over. When he finally found a small bundle of old envelopes, Schulz and I couldn't contain ourselves anymore. We flipped out. We grinned and cackled. I think we even kissed each other, which somehow made perfect sense under the circumstances and somehow wasn't gay. Eric tore open the envelopes, slashing them into pieces, greedily, angrily, until finally he found one with a stack of blue bills inside. My hands were covered in dust and dirt, and the parchment-like paper of the bills slid haltingly over my fingertips. Schulz dug into the bundle, grinding it.

Sam ran back to the hallway, almost tripping over Eric.

"W-w-what is it?"

Just like before, Eric threw the money up in the air. Only this time, it wasn't just a few bills. Dozens of hundred-mark bills fluttered down through the stale air. They fell to the floor like autumn leaves. Outside, summer began.

FIVE

I wanted to get going. But before I did, I counted the bills again. I'd been doing that a lot lately. It was fun. (Except for the fact that the paper smelled like old people and stuck to my fingers.)

It was Friday evening, a little after seven. I'd talked to Sam on the phone a couple of hours earlier. He'd sounded stressed out, like he was in a hurry; his sentences were short and clipped. He'd said that he was at home in bed, smoking weed, and that there was going to be a "session" at Daniel's house later. Sam never used the word "party"; it was always a "session." Daniel's parents were on vacation, and Eric had been staying there since the day before.

I'd tried to tell Sam that I was feeling guilty about the whole thing, and I could understand why he was stressed: Standing up to Eric was impossible. Eric was completely unwilling to give any ground in a disagreement. But Sam kept insisting that we needed to lay low and "keep quiet." "Just keep quiet," he kept saying. To him, that was what mattered most. "Keep quiet," over and over again. He didn't stutter when he said it—and that was something new.

• ♦ ●

After leaving the house on Tuesday, after our second visit, we went to the grocery store and filled a shopping cart with beer, Oreos, Gatorade, and individual refrigerated pizzas. The pizzas were supposed to be microwaved, but we usually just ate them cold—they still tasted good that way. At checkout Sam had carefully handed the cashier a hundred-mark bill. Without hesitating, she'd put it into the register and counted out Sam's change. Afterward, we brought the shopping cart down to the half-pipe with us. For some reason, I really enjoyed the sound of the wheels as the cart clattered down the asphalt. The rattle was almost soothing, and the faster we went, the more hypnotic the sound became—so I kept pushing it faster and faster. Eventually Sam and I broke into a full run, and at the smallest bump in the road the cart kept threatening to tip over. It made us laugh. When we finally got to the half-pipe, it had started to rain, so we left the cart there and went home.

• ♦ ●

As I was counting up the bills, I suddenly remembered: I had found a letter among the leftover empty envelopes

46

after we'd divided up the money. I'd secretly taken it, and now it was sitting in my desk drawer. Up to that point it hadn't occurred to me to read it. I didn't have time now, so I put it in my bag, took five bills from the bundle, shoved them in my pocket, and headed out.

On the local train were some men in suits and ties and some pudgy middle-aged women.

No one spoke. The wheels knocked rhythmically against the tracks. *Tock-tock, tock-tock, tock-tock.* The silence of the passengers got on my nerves. The rain had stopped, and a slanted light from the west shone over fields of sprouting corn. *Tock-tock, tock-tock, tock-tock.* I picked out one of the men with a suitcase and stared at him. His head drooped limply while his wearied eyes scanned the columns of his newspaper. He wore a frayed tan sports coat, rimless glasses, and in the middle of his head yawned an abyss crisscrossed by a few glistening brown hairs. He looked ridiculous. He must have been in his midforties. He made me sad. *Tock-tock, tock-tock, tock-tock.* He also made me angry, sitting there in such utter mediocrity, reading the same stupid newspaper on the same train route at the same time every day, year after year after year. My parents were always trying to get me to read the newspaper. But newspapers were just thick layers of boredom: boring people writing about boring things, and all of it just intensified the boredom. And then one day all that boredom would just swallow everything up. That was what it really amounted to, if you were honest. I slid my hand into my pocket and rubbed the bills between my fingers like a magic lamp. *Tock-tock, tock-tock, tock-tock.* I remembered the letter again and took it out, but the train was starting to slow so I put it back in my pocket.

PHILIPP MATTHEIS

Daniel lived in a townhouse near the abandoned home. All
the front yards on his street had only enough room for a
couple of bushes. In the back, hedges demarcated a series
of tiny little plots for dads to go out and grill marinated
pork chops in the summer. When I rang the doorbell, Eric
opened the door to greet me, not Daniel. His figure filled
the entire doorframe. He stood on the doorstep, legs apart,
as if he were master of the house. There was a ketchup
stain on his T-shirt that somehow didn't make him look
ridiculous. Nothing ever made Eric look ridiculous, only
cool. With a generous movement he held out his hand,
welcoming me in. When he said my name, per usual, his
voice was quiet. "We're playing *Tekken*," he added, and
shuffled down the hallway toward the living room.

I heard Daniel snickering. Daniel was a runt, a little
leprechaun. Some people thought he was a late bloomer
and would eventually shoot right up. But we were in our
late teens now, and the growth spurt had yet to happen.
At seventeen, he was all of four feet, eleven inches. But
despite being vertically challenged, he was spared the
fate of so many other short guys: No one made fun of
him. How he did it was a mystery. Daniel got along
with everyone, from the punks to the Turks. Junior-year
girls liked him, and so did the seventh-grade girls who
wore too much makeup. Despite a sort of ratty appear-
ance, emphasized by his slightly crooked front teeth,
his face was attractive. His small body was tucked into
the corner of the black leather couch, his hands glued

48

to the controller, and from under his hat two glassy eyes peered briefly in my direction.

The glass coffee table—which usually played host to an organized assortment of his mom's women's magazines—was in total disarray. Small crumbs of tobacco surrounded Daniel's glass bong, and next to the bong was Eric's bud. Wu-Tang Clan played in the background. I dropped onto the couch and watched them play. Eric won every time.

After fifteen minutes, Daniel tossed his controller into the corner and pressed his face to the top of the bong. The sunlight sank down through the front yard, and now and then the doorbell rang. When it did, Eric would get up, open the door, and then shuffle back to the couch. Daniel would give a quick nod to the guests, but otherwise he made no effort to greet newcomers. At least two hours went by like this. When the space on the couch and chairs was completely filled up and people were sitting on the floor with their beer bottles, Daniel suddenly jumped up and chanted for alcohol in a shrill voice: "Booze, booze, booze!" He ran like a weasel into the kitchen and returned with a bottle of vodka.

Sam, for his part, had brought two bottles of tequila. He opened one up and started drinking as if it were Coke. After the fifth gulp, he tore the bottle away, coughed, and spit up a liquor-saliva mixture onto the floor. In the corner, three guys in puffy jackets laughed at him. Sam asked defiantly, "Got a problem?"

One of the puffy jackets stared at him. Sam stared back.

"Got a p-p-problem?" Sam asked again.

"No, do you?"

The puffy jacket made a move to get up. But just then Schulz put a hand on Sam's shoulder and took the bottle from him. The puffy jacket sat back down and returned to staring at the TV. I rubbed the bills in my pocket and waited for Sam or Schulz to say something. But we stayed silent. We'd been lucky, and now we shared a secret. Our pact was sealed with silence. We drank to that, passing the bottle around until it was two-thirds gone.

In the meantime, the house had filled up. Jonah—a punk who everyone called Jim—trudged over to the stereo in his half-laced combat boots. He started talking to Orhan, a Turkish kid who lived near the train station, about switching the music from Wu-Tang Clan to something by Bad Religion. He tried to be diplomatic: "Bad Religion is way more political than Wu-Tang Clan."

Orhan said he didn't really care about politics. Jim started ranting about repression under the capitalist conditions for labor production.

"You're an immigrant! The system is especially out to get you. They're just like the Nazis," Jim said. He began to talk himself into a rage—as he always did when he drank too much. "The government pretends it wants peace while they sell weapons to the third world. It's all about the money!"

At some point Orhan said, "Hey punk, I just wanna listen to Wu-Tang."

Orhan and the other Turks always called him a "punk" when he started to get obnoxious. Jim backed down at that.

Eric, meanwhile, was virtually stationary. He was playing *Tekken* against one of the puffy jackets. When that one lost, another puffy jacket tried, and another one after him. Eric stayed in. Ollie and Ben, two goths with long hair and long black leather coats, had taken charge of Daniel's dad's office and were trying to roll a huge joint using six rolling papers. In the kitchen, two junior-year girls were discussing which AP courses they were going to take next year. Tim, a total dumbass who always wore a button-down shirt underneath a preppy sweater, was attempting to make a White Russian. Lang, his anorexic friend, was helping. Before long, Tim was puking, like he did at every party, and I went upstairs. In Daniel's room, a couple of skaters were sitting on his bed watching a skating video.

I wanted to lie down, so I headed to Daniel's little sister's room. But as I was about to open the door, it was yanked open from the other side, and there was Lena standing with a mixture of shock and anger in her eyes. Maybe that was the reason we couldn't look away from each other—not for a while, anyway. We definitely stared for an abnormally long time. I was about to say something like "sorry"—I couldn't think of anything else—when she slipped past me with a sideways movement and ran down the stairs into the noise of the party.

The wall above Daniel's sister's bed was plastered with Backstreet Boys posters. Schulz was sitting on the purple bedspread, elbows on his knees, smoking a cigarette. The setting felt almost intimate, yet with all the childish things surrounding him, he looked like an aged cartoon character.

"What's up?" I asked.

"She's crazy," he said. "She wants us to take the money back. She says it's stolen and she thinks it's wrong."

"Wrong? How?"

"That's just what she said. She thinks nothing good can come of it. It's stolen and she doesn't want anything to do with it."

"She doesn't have to have anything to do with it. It's not like she was there."

"I wanted to give her three hundred marks. So she could buy shoes or whatever. I thought she'd be happy about it. But instead she starts yelling, 'I'm not a hooker.'"

"Where did she go?"

"No clue. And I don't care."

What was I supposed to say? I'd never had a girl-friend, or at least, not a real one. How was I supposed to comfort a friend when I had no idea what it was like to fight with your girlfriend?

I said, "Wanna go get a drink?" I didn't know if that was the right thing to say, but Schulz nodded anyway.

·♦♦

One half hour and five tequila shots later, Schulz's troubles had disappeared. Eric was standing in the kitchen, where Tim was now drinking Coke, telling the junior-year girls that he couldn't care less about his future and that he was just glad not to be at that crappy school anymore. He thought people like Mr. Lexer, the physics teacher, were psychopaths, or at least really messed up.

Schulz was standing next to me, and when he raised his arm, I saw a new watch on his wrist.

Behind me I felt something soft graze my elbow. When I turned around, I started. The something soft was a girl's breasts.

The girl said, "You're the one who was totally stoned the other day."

It was the girl from the gas station. She was a good head shorter than I was and looked up at me with sassy, almond-shaped eyes. Her whole face had something childlike about it. It was round and surrounded by thick, strawberry-blonde hair. My gaze wandered downward. The shape of her whole body matched her small, angelic face. She wore a red-and-white striped shirt that hung down over her jeans like a dress.

I said, "Maybe," and then, "Yeah."

"That was funny," she said, and told me her name was Carina.

"How do you know Daniel?" I asked. I couldn't think of anything better to say.

"Your speech is slurred," Carina said. I grabbed an unopened beer from the counter, while she continued, "I've known Danny forever. We were in first grade together. We've always gone to the same school."

I used a lighter to open the bottle. It worked on the fourth try. I wanted to take her beer and open it for her.

But she insisted on doing it herself, which I thought was cool because most girls can't do it. I took a drink and lit a cigarette. After two puffs, I felt dizzy.

"But now we don't really hang out anymore," she said. The sound of her voice made my ears ring. I threw my cigarette down the sink.

"Now he just gets stoned and plays video games all day."

I searched for something meaningful to say, but I only came up with splintered thoughts that I couldn't piece together.

Carina said, "That's why I don't really like smoking pot, because the people who do that seem like they don't do anything else."

The blonde hair. The red-and-white striped shirt. The breasts that had brushed against my arm. The money in my pocket. The dimple on her chin.

"Can we go sit down somewhere?" I asked.

"Sure," she said, and took my hand. Her hand was tiny, warm, and a little damp. I let my guard down; she would watch out for me. She led me through the crush of people in the living room—Sam was in there somewhere, swearing—to the patio, and we sat down on a pair of white plastic lawn chairs. There was a grill in front of us. I heard Carina saying the words "ex-boyfriend" and "relationship," then she listed the names of some bands before asking me, "Who do you listen to?" I took a deep breath and then exhaled.

Suddenly, I didn't want to talk anymore, just sleep (though I would have liked to have held her hand again). I reached into my pocket and felt raw paper. Just once, just this one time, I wanted to look at the bills, in public, for just a second or two. But when I pulled my hand out, my fingers weren't holding the bills. Instead, I saw the letter.

"What's that?" asked Carina.

SIX

"It's simple. I'm gonna buy a pound from Zafko, but he's only gonna charge me for three quarter-pounds. He told me he gets it from his guy for the price of two. So he's still getting a big cut. But whatever, let's say I buy a P for the price of three QPs. That's 200 marks an ounce! And around here, an ounce goes for at least 275! Do the math!"

Eric didn't wait for an answer.

"That's 1,200 marks per P—1,200 marks of profit! If it works, I'll buy twice as much next time."

Eric's face came uncomfortably close to mine. I tried not to flinch, but I did anyway. His breath stank because he hardly ever brushed his teeth.

"But you don't have that much money."

"Dude, I'll get it on comm."

I didn't know what "comm" was, but I didn't have the heart to ask. I waited for a few seconds, hoping Eric would explain.

"So first I have to make a small down payment, right? About 500, as a deposit. Zafko'll give me the bud, I'll sell it for him, and then give him the other 2,700. Then, when I've done it a few times, I'll be able to pay him everything up front. Always better not to have debts. But for my first time, this is perfect."

"But where are you gonna sell it? You can't just stand here at the station and sell it to freshmen gram by gram."

"Dude, obviously I'm not gonna sell it all by the gram. One person will want ten grams, someone else will want twenty. In Munich, in the park. And that's just at first, see? Eventually I'll do it like Zafko. People will sell for me. Then I'll just handle the big business."

I wasn't sure why I wasn't as excited as Eric, and maybe that was why I didn't keep asking questions. Maybe I was also tired of being a buzzkill. It had warmed up and I was sweating in my socks and my thick skater shoes. Eric had gotten two new piercings: A second stud had been added above the earring he already had, and the new stud in his left ear was glinting in the sun. Big headphones hung around his neck, and he had obviously decided to let his hair and his beard grow out.

Now that he'd stopped talking, his eyes wandered back toward the horizon, and his head tilted slightly up and to the side as he focused on a distant point. Eric could smoke more weed than anyone. Almost every day he showed up with something new: One time it was grass and he told us it was "White Widow," and the next week he might even get "Super Skunk." Once he'd had a beige-colored piece that threatened to disintegrate at the slightest touch. "Compressed Pollen," he'd told us. Once he'd even had a piece of "Afghan Black." He explained that you don't use a lighter on Afghan. Instead, you roll a piece of it gently between your thumb and forefinger. Then that goes into a joint. Eric said he got it all from Zafko. Zafko, the dealer with his own apartment out past the train tracks, in the high-rise where the Turks and the Yugoslavs all lived.

●'●●

It had been two weeks since the party at Daniel's. As always, Sam and I still met every day at the half-pipe. My wallet, which was attached to my belt loop with a chain, was always full. Small luxuries, which used to be valuable because I didn't have them, were now available to excess. Sometimes I bought way more candy than I could eat. I would either throw the leftovers away or give them to someone without saying anything. Sometimes I would feed coins into Frank's pinball machine until playing got boring. Sometimes we went to Ingrid at the small corner bar and ordered B-52s, dinky little cocktails made with Baileys and Kahlua, which were insanely syrupy. I always had a pack of cigarettes in my bag, and I still had a wad of dusty bills in my wallet. I wanted to get a PlayStation, but there was no way. My parents would've asked me where I got the money. So I was forced to waste it on small, insignificant things. And that took a lot less time than I'd ever thought possible. I was a little shocked when I counted up the money again: It had shrunk from the previous count of twelve bills to only six. Then again, maybe I wanted it to disappear quickly.

It was possible that the others felt the same way, but Sam wasn't talking much. Eric was completely absorbed in his plans and dreams about being a dealer. We hardly saw Schulz because he was spending more time with Lena than ever.

Since Eric had been staying with Daniel the past two weeks, and Schulz was with Lena so much, it was mostly just Sam and me getting pizza and playing pinball at Frank's. Sam was leaving his skateboard at home more and more often. "Don't feel like it" was all he said. It made me think of first grade, when Sam was new at school and didn't talk at all. To everyone else he seemed weird, but that was exactly the reason I liked Sam. Everyone else talked all the time.

Eric returned from his daydream to the concrete of the half-pipe.

"It's gonna go off without a hitch, I'm telling you. Just think about it. A pound. I need a month for that. And that's being conservative. Maybe just two weeks. But okay, let's just say a month. In another month I can sell the second P. And then I'll buy two. And with that, I'll double my profit. See? That comes to 2,400 marks of profit—2,400 marks! Do you know what we could do with 2,400 marks?"

I smiled, unsure what to say. I honestly didn't know what we could do with 2,400 marks that we hadn't done already, except eat even more pizza at Frank's and feed even more coins to the pinball machine.

"What's with you? Are you even listening? Together, we could pull this off. If we split up the work, we'll be in business even faster. Then maybe later we could get into acid and pills. Maybe even blow. There's some serious cash there. Zafko's just getting started with it. But sometimes he's . . ."

Eric stopped. Suddenly Sam and Schulz were standing in front of us. Eric had been talking so loudly we hadn't heard them coming. They snickered and I noticed that their eyes were as red as albino bunnies'. Schulz had started wearing his hair in a ponytail. The gold of his new watch glinted around his wrist. He wore it loosely, so that it clinked a little when we shook hands. But he wasn't pulling off his new pimp look at all; he just looked ridiculous.

"Schulz," said Eric in a friendly voice. Schulz stretched his arm up and the watch slid back.

"Sam," said Eric. Couldn't he just shake hands normally? It was so fake.

Sam was temporarily confused. "H-h-hey, E-Eric," he answered. He was wearing a wife-beater T-shirt with his beige baggy pants. If they'd been a little less bunched up around his waist, and if his arms had been a little more

PHILIPP MATTHEIS

muscular, Sam would have been a pretty decent replica of
a boy band member. He may have stuttered, but he wasn't
bad looking.

"You guys are blazed," said Eric.

They nodded, looking like two comic strip characters with permanent grins.

"Ready to go?" asked Sam. "The train leaves in
eight minutes."

We nodded and grabbed our stuff.

When we got to the platform, Schulz went to the
ticket machine. Sam called over to him, "Why don't you
ever just get a ten-trip ticket? Are you retarded?"

Two of the other people waiting on the platform
looked up, first at Schulz, then at Sam. Schulz thought for
a second, opened his wallet, and threw a handful of coins
into the machine. It began to light up, gave a chirp, and
then spat out a piece of paper, which Schulz pocketed before walking back to us.

"You m-m-moron, why do you just buy one-way
tickets?"

"What's your problem? Just let me buy the damn
ticket," said Schulz. "I can afford it."

"True," said Sam, unexpectedly forgivingly. "True!"
he said louder. And then he shouted down the whole platform: "Truuuuuuuuue! He can afford it!"

Now all the waiting passengers turned and looked at
him. An old lady shook her head. He wasn't acting very
cool, but it was still kind of funny. Eric kicked him in the
shin and said, "Dude, not so loud."

We got on the train and dropped into the soft pleather
seats, the kind that stick to your skin when it's hot. Sam

62

opened his backpack and pulled out a Corona wrapped in a brown paper bag. Eric put on his massive headphones, stroked his chin, and proceeded to stare dreamily out the window for the rest of the trip.

"How's it going with Lena?" I asked Schulz. As I said the words, I realized that my real motive wasn't to see how Schulz was doing, it was to find out about Lena.

"Fine," said Schulz.

"Cool," I said. "I mean, is she still mad?"

Schulz didn't answer. After a full minute, he asked, "Why should she be mad?"

"Well, you know, because back at Daniel's party, she . . ."

"Lena is always mad about something, if that's what you're wondering. It's nothing, just the way she is."

"I mean, at Daniel's party, you were fighting, and she just walked out."

"Sh-sh-she was super pissed," said Sam. "Because of the money, you said."

"She gets upset, then she calms down again. I bought her some perfume. Since then, everything's been fine."

"Cool," I said again. But there was nothing cool about it. I thought it was totally uncool for him to buy her off with perfume. It wasn't insulting, exactly, but it somehow fit with the way Schulz was going around like a pimp. It was shady. Shady was the right word.

"W-w-women," said Sam, grinning moronically. He took a gulp of his beer. "They can be so obnoxious sometimes. Th-that's just how they are."

Schulz nodded, bored, and I watched Eric, who was still engrossed in the passing cornfields. I tried to guess what he was thinking, but I hadn't gotten very far when the first signs of city life appeared through the windows.

"C-cool graffiti," said Sam. His stuttering commentary was getting on my nerves.

"Graffiti! Yes, Sam, that is g-g-graffiti," I mocked him.

Suddenly Eric ripped his headphones off his ears. "We gotta get out."

I didn't understand. We weren't supposed to get out for two more stations, where we would transfer to the subway toward downtown.

"Why?" asked Schulz.

"Don't ask. Out. Now! We have to get out!" He jumped up. The train had already been stopped for a few seconds. I saw three older men coming down the aisle. One wore an outdated leather jacket that was too warm for the weather. Another one had a small leather bag dangling from his belt. Sam spilled his beer as he jumped up. At the last second we escaped through the door, just as it whooshed closed. The train continued on without us.

"Ticket inspectors," said Eric and, despite the no-smoking sign next to him, lit a cigarette. When an old man glared at him, he blew the smoke emphatically in his direction.

"F-f-fucking f-f-fuck," stuttered Sam.

Eric put his headphones back on and once again transformed into the daydreamer he had been for the whole ride.

We got on the next train. When we got off at the downtown station, it was busy, but we knew where we were going, and we didn't need to talk.

When we came up the steps from the subway station, we were surrounded by a comforting chaos. Across from Footlocker, an Indian man was selling food. The sun was shining. A little farther down it smelled like tacos. The trees were in bloom. There were girls *everywhere*. And there it was up ahead at the corner: McDonald's. We bought Big Macs, McRibs, Chicken McNuggets, vanilla milkshakes, Cokes, fries, and Eric got an apple pie. We ate. We literally bought everything on the menu. We even bought four McRibs, even though the McRib is the shittiest sandwich at McDonald's, and no one besides Eric liked it, and he only liked it because he ate everything. Anyway, at that moment I understood for the first time what it meant to have lots of money. I mean, how many people can say they've gone to McDonald's and ordered everything on the menu?

Our destination was a store off a side street from McDonald's. It sold baggy pants, hoodies, shoes, T-shirts with marijuana plant designs, and skateboards. Before, whenever I'd managed to save enough from my paper route, I'd come with Sam or Schulz to buy a T-shirt for forty marks or a pair of pants on sale. A blonde girl with a soft oval face was always standing behind the counter. Her hair was gelled, and her bangs hung down over her forehead.

She wore big silver earrings and skater clothes. At home, there really were no girls who dressed this cool. The girls in the suburbs didn't even listen to any good music; they just went to school, studied, had boyfriends with cars, and weren't interested in anything else.

When we came into the store, she was sorting receipts. We weren't confident enough to say hi, so we just walked to the back of the store, where the pants and T-shirts were. Eric and I took some T-shirts off the rack, grabbed some hats, and found some other stuff, like belts and socks, that you normally wouldn't buy at a store like that.

Just as we were about to take it all to the register, Schulz asked, "Don't you want to try them on first?"

Eric shrugged and took his pile into the fitting room; I followed. Sunlight streamed in through a window facing onto the street. It was wide open, and there was no screen. Eric pointed to the street. I opened the door a crack and called for Sam to come over. He then went back to Schulz and whispered something to him. Schulz bought a T-shirt and then left the store. He waited on the street in front of the window, and soon pants, T-shirts, and a hoodie came flying out. Then Eric and I left the fitting room and paid for two pairs of pants and a belt, handing the girl the old bills. Sure, it was pretty stupid for us to steal clothes that we could afford to buy. But then again, they were the ones who put a window in a fitting room.

The blonde girl smiled as we left the store—we'd just given her more than I'd spent there the entire last year.

We smiled back and then headed down the street. Our backpacks were crammed with almost a thousand marks' worth of clothes.

Life was simple and we were the ones calling the shots. Anyone who told us anything else was either a liar or a loser.

SEVEN

I saw Carina again on a Saturday evening in early June. She was behind the counter at the gas station. We hadn't run into each other since the night of Daniel's party—a night that I couldn't really remember.

All I knew was that when I'd woken up the next morning, I was lying in a bathtub, in my underwear, but with my shoes still on. Apparently I'd used the shower curtain as a blanket, and it reeked of beer. Absolutely everything reeked of beer, and my mouth tasted like it had been used as an ashtray. I sat up. Lying next to me on the floor was Christopher, a kid from my class. He was naked except for a washcloth over his crotch. He smelled like puke. I looked for my pants and found them next to the toilet. I reached into the pocket. The bills and the crumpled letter were still there. I didn't bother trying to find my T-shirt. I went downstairs and almost tripped over Daniel's giant bong, which someone had left on the steps. I found my jacket in the coat closet at the bottom of a massive pile. I put it on, pulled the zipper up to my chin, and went home. I refused to think about the letter and whether anyone might have read it. I wanted to forget it.

* ● ●

Daniel's parents were still out of town, and Eric had really settled in. As a thank-you gift, he gave Daniel a pair of pants from the skater store. Of course, they were way too long for his dwarfish legs, but he wore them anyway. Actually, all his clothes were way too long for him, but it was a look he pulled off pretty well.

That Saturday night when I saw Carina again, we were hanging out at Daniel's. We'd run out of booze, and Sam and I had gone to the gas station to get some more.

As we walked in I heard a friendly yet annoyed voice say, "That'll be sixteen forty-nine." I'd hoped she wouldn't be behind the counter. Everything that had happened was so fuzzy; I couldn't remember even a single clear moment. I mean, trying to say something funny or charming when you're stoned is hard enough, but feeling all this pressure on top of that, it was too much to handle.

"Jack Daniels," Sam suddenly called to me from the next aisle over. "I'm getting two bottles of Jack Daniels." He paused. "And tequila. Tequila, too."

"Maybe beer, too," I said quietly, attempting to go unnoticed by Carina.

I went to the fridge for some Coronas. They were all sold individually, so I tucked three bottles under my left arm but then realized I couldn't carry any more that way. I didn't want to walk back and forth to the register carrying a few at a time, so I put one bottle in each of my pants pockets and filled my left arm with three more from the fridge. *This might work,* I thought. I picked up one last bottle in my right hand, but then my pants, which were so baggy they barely stayed up in the first place, started to head south. It wasn't going to work. Now she was watching me. I felt her stare. I was fucked. What was Sam doing? Why wasn't he coming to help me? Had I spoken too softly for him to hear me? Damn it. My pants slid lower, and in a few seconds they'd lose all traction and . . .

"Sam!" I called angrily.

"W-w-what?"

I had to grab my pants. As I did, one of the bottles I was pressing into my chest fell and shattered on the linoleum, surrounding me in a puddle of beer and glass.

"Shit! Forget it," I called.

Sam laughed. Then *she* came over. She was holding a garbage bag and knelt down in front of me to pick up the pieces of glass. I carefully transferred the beer bottles, one by one, back into the fridge. The important thing was not to let go of my pants as she was kneeling there picking glass out of the puddle. I finally grabbed the bottles out of my pockets, put them back, and pulled my pants up high, over my belly button.

When she was finished and saw my hands were free, she handed me the garbage bag.

"Here, hold this," she said.

Sam was standing in front of the magazine rack, paging through the latest issue of *Time*.

Sometimes Sam scared me a little, but then I'd go back to thinking of him as a big teddy bear. He could be so pleasantly stupid. Sometimes that made him obnoxious, and at those times I wanted to smack him on his buzz-cut head.

A trail of beer traced my footsteps as we made our way to the register. I dropped the bag in front of the counter. Carina scanned the three bottles of liquor Sam gave her. Without looking at us, she asked, "Are you going to Danny's? I was gonna stop by later."

Why would she want to come to Daniel's again? That would just complicate things even more.

But Sam said, "Yeah, we'll be there."

"Forty-nine eighty-seven," she said.

I wanted to get out, so I didn't think about it, just handed her a hundred. "Keep the change."

She looked at me questioningly.

"Yeah, yeah, keep the change. Keep the change. It's all good. For the beer and whatever. Sam, come on, let's go. Thanks again."

I took the bag with the liquor in one hand and clutched Sam's arm with the other. "Thanks!" she called after us.

Daniel's front door was unlocked. He and Eric were sitting on the couch with their controllers, playing *Tekken* and blowing the occasional puff of smoke toward the ceiling. Orhan, three junior guys, and a girl I didn't know were also there. Orhan was trying to show the guys his butterfly knife. When he realized the weapon was eliciting more scorn than amazement, he pulled his white hat farther down over his black curls and played with the knife by himself. It snapped open, it snapped shut, it circled his wrist and snapped shut, it turned in his fist and snapped open.

Sam and I sat down. He arranged the liquor bottles on the table, and I went to get glasses from the kitchen, which by now looked like it had been left in the care of a pack of raging alcoholics. Finally, in the farthest corner, I found the only things that were still clean: two eggcups. We chased two eggcups of Jack Daniels with two eggcups of tequila.

Two hours and many eggcups later, Carina arrived. She sat down next to Daniel, but I was convinced that she was watching me out of the corner of her eye.

She went into the kitchen. For some reason Lena popped into my mind, but only for a second. Thinking about her made me think about Schulz. And that made me think of his stories about where, when, and how often he slept with Lena. None of us wanted to hear it, but as annoying as it was, we were also all jealous.

With those images and stories in my mind, I followed Carina into the kitchen. She had her back to me and was talking to some random girl I didn't know. It was a risk, but sometimes you just have to get in there and go for it, not hesitate, and do what you want to do. You had to be a man. I grabbed her ass.

The girl she was talking to looked at me in absolute disgust as Carina whipped around. I grinned.

"What the fuck?" Carina demanded.

My grin evaporated. Somehow I hadn't expected that reaction.

"Well, I gave you fifty marks today," I said.

Her little fist hit me right in the nose.

EIGHT

Dear Mr. Mueller,

They threw rocks into our yard again yesterday. One almost hit Gertrude in the head. It was the children, those Schneider brats. And the Summers' short little boy was there, too. They hate us. The Schneider woman hisses at me when she sees me. In fact, they all hiss constantly. There is a constant hissing. They do it because they want to make our lives unbearable! They have hated us since the day we moved into this house. Gertrude is getting worse every day. She keeps saying that she cannot take it anymore. Please, you have to help us. Surely there is enough evidence now. Please, you are our last hope.

Sincerely,
Hilda Stetlow

After Eric had read the letter, he was quiet for a while, and then simply said, "Crazy." That was it. Then he went back to staring into space.

"They wrote this letter to their lawyer, but they never sent it. It's dated August 8, 1991. Why would someone do that?"

Eric shrugged. "It's crazy," he said. "Totally crazy. I have no idea why anyone would do that. No idea at all."

"Maybe someone stopped them from sending it."

"Hmm. Or they were just insane."

"What if they're still alive?"

"No way. They must be dead. Otherwise they would have taken their money with them." Eric stroked his chin in silence. After a while, I spoke up again: "Maybe they were taken away."

"Hmm." Eric stroked and stared.

"Don't you think it's kind of disturbing?"

Eric grunted, then abandoned his blank stare and turned to face me.

"Let's go to Frank's and get a pizza. I can't think straight when I'm hungry."

We were at the half-pipe, just Eric and I. We walked fast, Eric always a step ahead, so it took some effort for me to keep up.

"Don't you think it's disturbing?" I asked again.

"How?" He walked faster.

"Well, it's all just really strange. Disturbing, I mean. At least a little bit, anyway . . ."

"Maybe at first it's a little weird. But when you think about it, it's not. I mean, look, that's what business is. One group gets the thing they want, and the other group gets the thing they want."

"This isn't about business! It's got nothing to do with that."

"No, dude, it's business. Each person gets something out of it, so what's the difference? It's no different from us buying a pizza at Frank's."

I hated it when he walked ahead of me. Whenever he did it I always wound up looking pathetic. Either I ran after him like a pet dog, or else I had to ask him to go slower. Either way I looked like an idiot.

I tried to follow his logic. "Okay, so it's business. Obviously the lawyer gets something out of it. He gets money. Which they have plenty of."

"Exactly. Someone wants something, someone else gives it to them. I don't see the problem."

"Uh, that wasn't the problem I was talking about." I was panting. "I'm just wondering why they didn't send the letter."

Eric stopped in his tracks.

"What letter? And what kind of lawyer are you talking about? I don't need a lawyer. I'm not gonna get caught!"

"The letter from the house! The letter you just read! It was addressed to a lawyer."

"Oh, right, that letter." Eric turned around and continued marching at almost a jogging pace.

"So what do you think?"

"No idea. Honestly, I really don't care who was upset with who. That was forever ago. I was talking to Zafko again yesterday. Just talking—not about selling his stuff and getting commission. Though that's definitely getting started soon. I can get going with it whenever. But I just asked him, all casual, 'So, what if I bought a whole pound?' He laughed at me and said, 'Forget it. You could never afford it.' I stared back at him and said, 'Or maybe I could.' I said it just like that. He gave me this look— you should have seen it. And so I asked him again, 'How much would a pound cost if I bought it direct?' He didn't know what to say! He just stared at me for a minute. Then he told me: 'Three thousand marks.' So maybe I'll do it, bring him the cash. Work for him? Fuck that shit. That's stupid. If I'm going to do this, it's way better for me just to go big."

A breeze swept past us, making the hairs on my arm bristle. It felt good on such a humid evening. The red sun was just sinking below the supermarket in the distance. I didn't like June. Too much growing and blooming. I was tired and sweaty, but Eric—Eric, the Energizer bunny— just kept going.

"Eric, maybe this is a dumb question, but . . ." Something was blocking my train of thought. Something to do with Sam.

Eric didn't turn around or slow down. He just muttered, "Huh?"

"Are . . . aren't you worried?"

"Worried?"

"Yeah, worried. About getting caught. About not being in school. I mean, aren't you worried about the future or whatever?"

He stopped in his tracks. The last rays of sunlight were reflected in his eyes. He looked straight at me, as if he were going to fight me right there in some struggle for the truth. I couldn't hold his gaze. I felt ashamed the second I looked away. It's always the losers who look away first.

Then Eric spoke. "My dad said something like that to me the other day. He's always talking like that. He said, 'Son, what do you want to do with your life? Remember when you were ten, when you wanted to go to college and become an archaeologist? Now you've gotten yourself kicked out of school, you're on drugs, and you're going nowhere fast.' I know exactly why he talks to me like that. He's checking to see if he can still pressure me into doing what he wants. He knows he can't really stop me. I don't live with him. I take care of myself. So he's trying to play mind games. But he can go fuck himself. That shit doesn't work on me. They can all go fuck themselves. All of them. I don't need them, and they don't need me either."

Then he took off again, slower than before, but with the same intensity. His head was bent forward, like he was fighting gale-force winds instead of a pleasant summer breeze. He spoke again.

"That money is ours. We're untouchable now. And I'm not gonna just blow it on nothing. I'm gonna invest it. That money from the house is just seed money. Give it three years, okay, maybe five, and we'll probably be millionaires." I'd never heard him speak so fast. "What do I need school for? Why do I need to graduate? Sure, college might be fun. But I can read books on my own. I don't need school for that. Look, right now I'm reading this book called Chariots of the Gods. I read a little every day. It's really interesting. Did you know that the pyramids in South America and the ones in Egypt are insanely similar? There's no way humans could have built something like that. This guy says—and this is so awesome, just think about it—he says it was aliens. How are you gonna learn stuff like that in school?"

♦♣

I ordered a pepperoni and sausage pizza and Eric got his calzone again. Frank plunked the steaming boxes onto the counter. "Nine marks," he grunted.

Eric pulled a crumpled hundred from his pocket and tossed it on top of the boxes. Frank took the money, and it disappeared into the black recesses of the register. As he counted out Eric's change, I thought I saw him cast each of us a quick, scowling glance. But he didn't say anything.

We sat outside on the stone steps, which were still warm after the hot day, and stuffed ourselves as twilight fell. Honestly, I was starting to get tired of pizza. It was still good, but it wasn't a special treat now. It was just a greasy clump of cheese with oregano. Nothing more.

"Do you fink . . ." I asked Eric with my mouth full. "Do you fink that Fwank . . ." I forced myself to swallow a lump of cheese so big it almost hurt. "Do you think Frank's noticed anything?"

"Who? Lardass? Hell no, he's happy to have some regular customers. Doesn't matter to him where the money comes from." Sauce dribbled out of the corner of Eric's mouth. He wiped it onto the back of his hand and slurped it off.

"How many times have you been here the past few days?"

"How many? No clue, maybe every other day. Or maybe every day."

"Every day?" Before, we used to have to save up all our change just to be able to afford a single pizza at the end of the week. "You've gotten a calzone every day? Do you always pay with hundreds?"

"Not always. But if I don't have any change on me, yeah, I pay with a hundred. It doesn't matter. Get a grip, you sound paranoid. Not everything is about us."

"What if we get caught?"

"Juvie. It's not that bad. Or you'd get community service and have to change diapers at a home for the handicapped. I had to do that once. It's not that bad."

⁕ ⁂ ⁑

We walked back to the half-pipe after dark. Pebbles crunched underneath our shoes as we went. In the distance we saw the lights from a train. When we were almost to the concrete blocks, we saw something glowing. It was just a small point that would get brighter, then almost go out, only to light up again right away. The ember wandered a little, lit up, and then dimmed again.

Sam was sitting cross-legged on the ground with Schulz. Schulz was smoking a joint. Eric was the first to reach them.

"Sam!" He went to grab Sam's hand energetically, but Sam just held out a limp fist and stared up at him.

"Schulz! What's up?"

Just then the train thundered over the tracks. It was loud enough to drown out our voices—or at least it would have been, if Sam and Schulz had been saying anything. Instead, Schulz just handed Sam the joint and they looked at each other. They seemed to be waiting for something. The flame had gone out and Sam had to relight the joint.

Then Schulz lifted up his head, and we saw it: His left eye was swollen shut, like a boxer's after a fight.

"What's that?" asked Eric.

"Are you blind? What do you think it is? It's a black eye, that's what. It's what you get when some asshole smashes your face in." He really launched into Eric, but when he finished talking, his head sank back down.

"Yeah. I can see it's a black eye."

"They punched him in the jaw, too," Sam blurted out, and then immediately stuck the joint back between his lips. He reminded me of a baby with a pacifier.

"Who? Who punched you? Who was it?"

"Yeah, who?" I asked. I wanted to say something, too.

"S-S-Strasser."

"Strasser? Strasser, that jackass who's always at the sports bar?" Eric knew Strasser from when they were little and their families lived in the high-rises on the other side of the tracks. Eric still hated him because Strasser used to beat him up a lot in grade school.

"That's the one. This afternoon, on my way home. He and his douchebag friends headed me off at the train station." Schulz seemed like he was enjoying the attention, maybe even milking it a little.

"I was going through the tunnel, and suddenly there he was. I wanted to just get past him, so I was like, 'Hey, Strasser.' Then he shoved me and said he wanted my money. I said, 'What the hell? I don't have any money.' I dodged the first punch. But then . . . I think I got him once . . . I think. And then his two bitches came, that fat kid Riedler and this other guy, I don't know what his name is. I didn't stand a chance. If he'd been alone, I swear I would've kicked his ass. But one against three? I didn't have a chance! No one would." Schulz's voice was shaky as he added a quiet, "Right?"

We all knew that Schulz, thin and fragile as he was, never had a chance against Strasser. But we kept quiet, our silence communicating our support.

"It's just so fucked up. Three on one! You have no idea what it feels like. It's just so cowardly. If it had just been one on one . . . then I would've . . ."

"Schulz," I interrupted. "Why? Why did he come to you for money?"

"Don't know. He just said, 'Give me your money!'"

"Is that exactly what he said?"

"He said, 'I heard you got some money.'"

"'I heard you got some money'?" I repeated.

"M-m-money," repeated Sam.

"It doesn't fucking matter what he said. Look at my eye! I can barely see anything. It'll be a good three weeks before the swelling goes down. I have to go around like this for three weeks! I look like shit!"

"But after they beat you up, what happened then?"

"The sons of bitches stole my watch. My new watch! Fucking assholes!"

Eric, who had remained silent through all of this, suddenly rose up. Sticking out his chest, he tensed his neck muscles and balled his hands into fists. He looked almost animalistic.

"I'm gonna end him. *We're* gonna end him. Listen: We can't let this happen to us. We can't let him get away with it. Strasser's the last son of a bitch that screws with us!" He enunciated the last syllables like a military command.

"Y-y-yeah!" shouted Sam.

"I'm gonna talk to Orhan tomorrow. He's got a score to settle with Strasser, too. All the Turks will definitely want to help us. And they know how to use their knives. I know for a fact that Orhan's cousin stabbed someone once."

But Schulz wasn't so enthusiastic. "I don't know what that would accomplish. Strasser has people, too. It's not going to accomplish anything." He looked at the concrete in front of him and hung his head.

Then suddenly Sam chimed in off-handedly. He said, "Maybe Strasser knows about the house."

We looked at each other. Schulz with his busted eye, Eric with his bloodthirsty stare, me with my clenched jaw, and Sam, looking like an overly enthusiastic yet violent comic book character.

At first no one said anything.

"There's no way!" Eric said. He lit another cigarette, and I felt in my pocket for the bundle. "There's no way. He can't know about it. How would he?"

No one answered his question. Sam looked at the ground, which made him look really suspicious. Maybe *he* had told someone about it. Maybe it wasn't my fault after all. I hadn't told anyone about what had happened at Daniel's party, not even Sam. Besides, Carina . . . she . . . she hadn't been interested in any of it. Maybe she had read the letter, but I definitely hadn't said a word about the money.

"Sam?" asked Eric, in a way that sounded like Chuck Norris. "Did you tell anyone?"

"No. No one. I d-d-didn't say anything. N-not a word. I s-swear." Sam spoke so quietly we could hardly hear him.

"What about L-L-Lena?" Sam asked. He sounded suddenly aggressive, which surprised Schulz. "Lena knew about it from the beginning. Y-you told her everything!"

"She's my girlfriend, of course I'm gonna tell her about it. I . . . I have to tell her. But she . . . she keeps her mouth shut. I know she does. What are you saying, asshole?"

"H-h-how can you be so sure? Sh-sh-she doesn't like Eric, she doesn't like me, but she does like guys with their own cars. How do you know she didn't tell someone?"

"Because she's my girlfriend, damn it!" Schulz shouted. "Because she wouldn't do that. And what the hell do cars have to do with anything? I don't have a car. Anyway, what about you guys? Daniel knows, doesn't he?" Schulz looked at Eric. "And Jonathan, you were so stoned at Daniel's party that you can't remember anything about it, you said so yourself. Maybe you told someone while you were shit-faced. Leave Lena out of it, damn it! I trust her, all right? I trust her . . ." He shook his head.

"I didn't say anything," I said quietly.

Then we fell silent and smoked. The train thundered over the tracks. It got quieter, the night got darker, the smoke from our cigarettes curled through the air. I found the constellation Orion, the only one I knew.

"We gotta go back in," said Eric quietly but resolutely, as if he was simply stating a truth that could not possibly be discussed further.

"W-w-what?" asked Sam.

"We gotta go back in. We can't take the risk that someone else knows about the house and might find more money in it."

"Are you crazy? It's way too dangerous right now. Strasser knows about the house, and probably other people do, too," I said. "What about all the people who might have noticed something? Like Frank. Have you noticed how he's been suspicious of us? What if someone tells the cops? What if we get caught?"

In the last few days we hadn't talked about the house at all. Once, I'd mentioned it to Sam, who used to talk about it a lot. But this time he just said, "Lips zipped," making the motion with his fingers, and snickered.

"You don't get it!" said Eric. "If someone knows about the house, they're gonna want to go in and get the rest of the money. No one's gonna go to the police when they have the chance of finding a few thousand marks. The only question is who it's gonna be. Us, or Strasser and his friends."

"I don't know," said Schulz. "I think Jonathan is right. It was cool at first, but now it's getting dangerous."

"Schulz," Eric said pleadingly. "Schulzie, just think for a second. We'll go inside just one more time and clean the place out. An afternoon, a half hour, and we'll really look. There's more in there. You don't need to get your watch back from Strasser. You'll get a new one. Or would you rather that Strasser got the cash?"

"So maybe Strasser or someone else knows that we found money," I said. "But they have no way of knowing where the house is. There are hundreds of houses in this town."

"Strasser's a douchebag, but he's not stupid," Eric said to me. "I know him, I went to grade school with him. He just has to start asking around about abandoned houses. I'm telling you, we have to get in as fast as possible and get the money. It's much safer that way." He turned to face all of us. "You know, it's much safer if it's just the four of us getting the money than if lots of people know about it. Just think about what would happen if Strasser got the money. Those guys can't keep their mouths shut . . . If they know about the house, you might as well start handing out flyers. It's gotta be us! No one else!"

"All right, fine," said Schulz. "You're probably right. Strasser's a fucking asshole. It's our house and our money."

I asked, "You think there's still more money inside?"

"There has to be more. We didn't look very hard, and we still found five thousand marks," said Eric.

My stomach tightened. I asked, "So when do we do it?"

"Tomorrow afternoon."

"Tomorrow afternoon?"

"Tomorrow afternoon."

We nodded.

Sam, however, remained silent.

NINE

That night, I brushed my teeth, got into bed, and smoked a cigarette. The dark blue of the cigarette pack has always appealed to me, but the cigarettes themselves were actually pretty terrible. The window was open and everything—the smoke, the cigarette pack, my skin, the walls—shimmered dark blue.

I tried to imagine who this Hilda Stetlow person was. I tried to imagine what she was like. And how she had wound up with all that money.

She's sixty-five years old and kind of lumpy. It's hard to imagine a Hilda who doesn't spend every day in a colorful shift dress, with her gray hair pulled tight in a high bun, which unravels and gets messier and messier over the course of her day's work. She's a good-natured woman, but in her old age she has also become a bit senile. She smiles a lot—often because she's happy, but more often because she's confused. Everything about her—her face, her body, her bun—is round.

The effort that she has to put in to keep up the house and care for her sister has become almost overwhelming. Of course, she's still able to finish everything before the day is over, but it doesn't come to her as easily as it did several years back. Now, in the evenings, when she finally sinks into bed, she is completely drained. Sometimes when her sister calls for help at night and Hilda gets up to go to her, she finds herself thinking a terrible thought, and the only cure she knows of is to cross herself. She wishes that her ailing sister would die.

Every time she makes the sign of the cross over her chest, she can't help thinking, "If only my son were here! Everything would be different if he were here instead of in America." She has no idea what he does for a living. But she would much rather have him with her than the hundred dollars he airmails over every month. She always saves the money for a full year, and then shortly before Christmas she drives to Munich and exchanges them for marks. She has done that for years. Hilda Stetlow doesn't trust banks; they feel threatening, so instead of opening a savings account, she hides the bills in every corner of her house. She puts them aside for a rainy day. But that rainy day never comes, and so year after year, the pile of hundred-mark bills keeps growing . . .

I'd always thought moonlight was corny, or else something for people who didn't have streetlights. But at that moment, a silver light fell into my room. The atmosphere was thrilling. I remembered the crumb of hashish still lying in my pants pocket. There was enough for one pretty sizeable joint—all for me.

After I smoked up, though, I started to feel anxious. I couldn't think straight, and my image of Hilda Stetlow began to morph. The stout, rotund lady became a haggard, wiry figure . . .

Her bun is frayed, with the hairs sticking out wildly around her wrinkled face. Her dress is covered with stains: coffee, ketchup, and little bits of cereal. It smells. She smells. Everything about her is chaotic.

She shuffles through her garbage-strewn apartment, opens drawers, leaves food out, and hides money. Her lawn becomes overgrown, and the bushes sprawl over the fence, onto the street, and into the neighbors' lawns—which leads to a lot of drama, of course. Something changes in Hilda Stetlow. Something's wound her up, and now she's like a ticking time bomb that could explode at any moment. Her neural pathways have been corroded from years of abusing prescription drugs; she's become vicious.

As the moonlight shone on my face, I put out the joint in the ashtray and let my head fall heavily back onto my pillow.

Then one day, Stetlow captures the Summers's cat on one of its forays into her yard. She tortures it, kills it, and buries it in her own basement.

The process of burying the animal is conveniently aided by the fact that the basement has no floor—since Hilda Stetlow, driven by her absurd cheapness, stopped payment on the renovations. The rumor makes the rounds quickly: nasty old Stetlow—that witch—killed pets and kept the dead animals in her basement. Grown-ups whisper when they saw the old woman, children cry, "Witch, witch!" and run away from her, half in fear, half in joy at the thrill of it. When the children yell at her, Hilda Stetlow hisses back.

Then, one day, Stetlow takes a few too many pills. Her heart pounds in her chest; her thoughts race through her head; she could hardly stay upright on her own two feet. Everything is horribly bent and distorted, like a spring that has been extended beyond its breaking point; she feels strained to the utmost, about to shatter. She goes out into the street, wearing only her dirty shift dress. Everything around her—the asphalt on the street, the hedges in the yards, and the walls of the neighboring houses—is bent, as if they are under an enormous weight. Hilda Stetlow could see the end coming.

"♦♦

The phone rang.

I jumped, disoriented. After the third ring, I finally managed to emerge from my coma-like state and peel myself out of my bed; after the fifth, I picked up the receiver, shivering.

"Hilda?"

"Are you serious?"

". . ."

"What? Who's Hilda?"

"Nothing, sorry, I just woke up."

"It's eleven thirty."

"Yeah, exactly," I said.

"What time do you go to bed? I'm never asleep before twelve."

"I, uh, I don't know, Lena. Normally around one." That was a lie; I hardly ever went to bed after twelve, but that would've made me sound pretty damn lame.

"Around one? But it's only eleven thirty now." With just a few quick questions, she'd managed to reveal me as a liar, even to myself. In the space of two sentences she somehow made me feel guilty. It made me think of Schulz. She must do the same thing to him. Schulz . . . me . . . I pulled myself together.

"So . . . what's up? Did you just call to talk about the ideal bedtime?"

"I thought you'd be glad I called."

"Yeah, of course I'm glad, but . . ."

"Doesn't sound like it. Whatever, it doesn't matter now."

"What? What doesn't matter? Of course I'm glad when you call. I'm always glad when you call me. It's just . . . I was just sleeping, and I had this really weird dream."

"About Hilda."

"Yeah, about Hilda. Wait, it's not what you think. Hilda's not . . . whatever, it doesn't matter. So whatever, I . . . wait, don't change the subject. You're the one who called me."

Lena giggled. It sounded tinny through the receiver, but it made me feel good; it was sweet.

"What's so funny?"

"Nothing, you're just cute."

"Cute?"

"Yeah, kind of adorable."

"Ah."

I felt flattered—even though I was pretty sure she wasn't just saying it to be nice. She had some ulterior motive, but I didn't know what it could be. Maybe she even knew that I knew something was up. It didn't matter though. It didn't change anything.

"Yeah, so, what's up?"

"You want to go back there. Into the house again."

"No. No way. I mean, that's not exactly true. Anyway, who told you that?" Of course, Schulz must have told her, and it was completely ridiculous for me to try to lie about it. I stopped talking.

"He just told me about it. We had a fight."

She didn't speak again for a long time, and I didn't say anything either. No matter what I said, it wasn't going to change anything.

"Look. I'm sorry to wake you up. It's just . . . sometimes I just need someone to talk to. I don't know what else to do."

I didn't say anything.

"I don't know why, but with you, I always feel like you understand me. I . . . I didn't want to bother you, I just don't know what else to do sometimes. I . . ."

She sniffled. Once, then twice, then everything swelled to a sob, and that was more than I could take.

"Lena." I was startled by my voice because it came out in a whisper. "Please don't cry. What happened? You can tell me everything, really. I'm wide awake now, I'll listen. Please stop crying. Everything'll be okay." And then I said it: "He's not worth it."

Her sobbing stopped, as if she had been waiting for those words. I heard her sniffling.

"He's an idiot," she said and sniffed her nose.

"An idiot," I repeated.

"He doesn't deserve me," she said.

"He doesn't," I repeated.

"And he's really not that good looking."

"You wanted to tell me what happened."

She laughed again, which made me happy, but at the same time it seemed a little messed up. I mean, how could she be crying one second and laughing the next? Anyway, she told me what happened.

When Schulz went home after leaving the half-pipe, Lena came over to his place. She started getting on his case about his black eye. She told him, "Everything that happens to a person is a result of his own actions, and if you got a black eye, then you did something to deserve it." She'd just been reading about that in some philosophy book. At some point Schulz flipped out. He threw his PlayStation controller against the wall and screamed at her. He said he didn't need anyone who "wasn't 100 percent" supportive. Lena started to cry and said, "It's all because of the money. It's brought bad luck." Schulz yelled, "Money, my ass! You liked when I bought you that shitty perfume. And this is the thanks I get?"

Lena told him that wasn't true, that he didn't understand anything. Then Schulz said, "Just wait and see. You'll be hot for me again tomorrow. We're getting more money tomorrow."

Lena told him that lately he's seemed more and more like a loser who needs money to boost his self-confidence.

Then Schulz called her a "whore."

Lena said that then she stood up in front of Schulz and slapped him before she could control herself. She meant to hit his cheek, but instead her hand met Schulz's eye.

Schulz winced, and she immediately said she was sorry. She said, "Sorry, Schulzie," and went to comfort him. But Schulz didn't act like he'd heard her at all. He just hit her back.

* ♦ ♣

Lena was crying again. I didn't know what to say to comfort her. I wanted to say that it was definitely not okay to hit a girl. Not under any circumstances, friendship or not. You just didn't do that. Maybe I even wanted to tell her that I couldn't still be friends with Schulz anymore. But I didn't say any of that.

Instead I just said, "Shit."

•❦•

A dog is walking down a street. On either side of him
are manicured lawns and long driveways that end with
unforgiving brown garage doors. His feet go "tep-tep-
tep" over the hardened tar of the street. Yards are taboo;
the dog knows that. And so he trudges on down the
street, hungry, thirsty, tired. His tongue hangs out of his
mouth. His paws are blistered from the hot, raw asphalt,
and every now and then a small pebble will bore into them.
There's not a dog, person, or cat in sight, nothing but asphalt and houses, nothing to engage his senses, no smell,
no sound. Only the eternal monotony of the never-ending
row of identical houses with their forbidden yards and the
soft whisper of his own four paws on the asphalt. Tep-
tep-tep-tep, tep-tep-tep-tep, tep-tep-tep-tep . . . Suddenly
something appears on the horizon. The street is a dead
end, and the dog has a destination. He breaks into a trot
and a scent creeps into his nose. He goes faster, the rhythm
of his paws' patter accelerating, tep-tep-tep-tep-tep-tep.
He smells meat. His muscles vibrate; everything in him
starts to pull in one and the same direction. The monotony
of the street, the forbidden houses and yards, they become
like guardrails guiding him along the way. The scent of the
dead flesh streams through his brain and his eyes seek out
the destination, a tantalizingly red gleaming pile. There is
no doubt anymore, not a hint of reluctance, no distrac-
tion, everything is clear. With all the strength that his jaws
can muster, he lunges into the moist flesh. Panting and
grunting, he tears out a big chunk, twisting his head

around to gather enough force. There's only him and the meat. He eats.

Several minutes later, he's dead. But his poisoned body continues to twitch in the afternoon sun.

• ♦ ♠

The red digits on my clock read 5:46 a.m. when I woke up. I felt sick and I remembered the pepperoni and sausage pizza at Frank's. I went to the bathroom and briefly glanced in the mirror. I should explain that I don't like mirrors: In malls, in train stations, or even in fitting rooms, I always try to avoid them. I have a picture of myself in my head, and in it I look okay. I don't need to constantly inspect whether everything is perfect. But now, there was no helping it: My hair was sticking out all over the place and my eyes were marbled with red. I thought it would be terrible to have a job where you had to get up this early every day.

TEN

Sam looked like a ninja. He had a blue bandanna wrapped over his mouth and nose. Only his eyes were visible between the square of fabric and his Yankees hat. He was wearing wool gloves "in case of fingerprints or whatever."

When Schulz took off his new Ray-Bans, I could see that the swelling around his eye had gone down, but now a purplish-reddish-bluish bruise extended from the bridge of his nose all the way to his temple. "These aren't knock-offs," he said, pointing to the sunglasses.

It was a bright day. The sun blazed through the hazy blue afternoon sky, making Eric blink when he looked at it. In a way, it seemed like he was almost communicating with the heavens above. I'm sure he was thinking about something from *Chariots of the Gods*. The pants that he had stolen from the skater store were already ripped at the ends because they fell past his shoes, and he was always stepping on them. He took a final drag from his cigarette and threw it on the sidewalk. Then he sucked in the summer air, his nostrils flaring a little as he did. He looked wild, almost like an animal. Once again Eric was the first one to jump over the fence gate, which was now almost completely overgrown by the hedge. We followed after him.

A bee buzzed lazily above the dandelions and knee-high grass. We opened the patio door and breathed in the mildewed air as we stepped inside. We felt like pros. We knew the ropes now. We went up the steps instinctively, without saying a word to one another. The plywood door on the second floor was open, just like the last time. We were in.

We spread out right away. Sam headed to the back, toward the living room, where the balcony was. Schulz went into the kitchen. (I could hear plates rattling as he threw open the cabinet doors.) Eric and I went into the bedroom.

Eric pulled out the drawer in the nightstand and dumped the contents onto the floor. Rings and bracelets rapidly disappeared into his huge pants pockets. I pushed the mattress up a little, stooped down, and laid it on my right shoulder. No one said a word; we were like a SWAT team carrying out a search warrant. We had a solid routine. In the middle of the bed frame I saw a bundle of envelopes. I extended my arm as far as I could, but my fingers still couldn't reach and the mattress was heavy on my shoulder. Suddenly the mattress bent. Eric pushed it up.

"Fuck that," he said.

We pulled the mattress out of the frame, balancing it against the wall, and leafed through the pile. The unsealed envelopes, smelly with age, contained letters that had never gone out. But they didn't have any money.

"Schulz, get us a knife!" Eric called. A moment later, a figure with sunglasses and a slightly rusted chef's knife stood in the doorway. Schulz grinned.

"You look like someone from *Dead Alive*," said Eric. "Give me that thing."

Schulz didn't give it up. He held it tight in his hand, not relaxing his grip—or his grin. He came toward us slowly, deliberately, and then mounted the mattress and stabbed it. The knife tore into the padding, so deep you couldn't even see the blade anymore. Then Schulz dragged it down, stopping after about four inches. He pushed his hand in and felt around in all directions until eventually his entire lower arm had disappeared inside.

I was sure that he was about to produce gold or at least a bundle of hundred-mark bills. But after a minute, as Schulz kept rummaging around in the moldy thing, I couldn't help but think of Andy Stattler. Someone at school had told us about how Stattler, after losing some bet, had to go stick his arm up a cow's butt. So one night Stattler and his friends snuck into a barn. His arm was in the cow up to his elbow when suddenly the lights came on and the farmer was standing there armed with a pitchfork. Stattler had left school at least five years ago, but the rumor stuck around.

"Schulz, I don't think there's anything in there," said Eric.

"Yeah, there is," he wheezed. "I mean, there's gotta be *something*." His entire body struggled against the weight of the mattress.

"I think we would have spotted a seam somewhere."

In the meantime, I took a couple of letters from the pile and shoved them into my pocket. Sam appeared in the doorway and stared at the crazy dude with half an arm waving around inside a shredded mattress.

"There's nothing out there," he said, like a soldier reporting back from his latest patrol.

Finally, Schulz gave up and pulled his arm out of the mattress. A thick wire spring followed him. His face was bright red. "Shit," he said. "What if there's nothing else here?"

"Chill out," Eric said. "There has to be something."

With that, we collectively scanned the room in silence—four pairs of eyes hunting for treasure. Four brains pondering where the best hiding place would be. We all stopped at the same place.

The wardrobe.

Eric took two quick steps and stopped only inches away from its hulking darkness. It was over six feet high and six feet wide, with smooth, rounded edges. Its doors were locked.

"Where's the key?" asked Eric, boring his fingertips into the narrow opening between the door and the bolt. He pushed, tore, and yanked at it as hard as he could. The old wood creaked but the wardrobe didn't open. "There has to be a key here somewhere. Damn it. Those assholes must have hidden a key somewhere."

Schulz pulled the rug back from front of the wardrobe, spraying dust everywhere; he coughed asthmatically as the giant cloud enveloped his face. Eric got a chair from the kitchen, stepped up on it, and felt with his hand over the top of the wardrobe. Eric yanked at the door again. His fingers slid along the length of the upper edge of the wardrobe door until they found a hold at the corner. Sam kneeled on the floor in order to yank at the lower edge at the same time. The wood groaned, and the door bowed outward at the corners. Schulz and I came to help; both of us grabbed hold of tiny openings in the middle. The four of us pulled and bent the stubborn old door. We swore and grunted. Then Eric stopped, got down from the chair, pushed it aside, and moved a good three feet back from the wardrobe. We shifted aside, and Eric rammed into it once, twice, three times. But the wood didn't break.

I ran downstairs to the first floor. I remembered the ax leaning against the wall in the big room with the clothing line. I savored the weight of the steel, which strove toward the ground even as I heaved it up. I ran my fingers over the cold metal, felt the small grooves in the blade, slid my hand back over the warm wood to the handle. Armed now, I went back upstairs into the bedroom.

When the others saw me, they paused. I didn't let go of the weapon. I had found it and I wanted to be the one to use it. I smiled, and everyone stepped aside.

The ax arced upward and sped down into the hardy old wood. It cracked. Splinters shot into the air like sparks.

"Awesome!" cried Sam.

But the ax was stuck. I pulled it down, pulled it up, and yanked on it with both hands until the steel finally dislodged from the wood. Then the hatchet fell a second time. A third time. The dark wood began to split.

"Finish him!" Eric bellowed, echoing the famous line from one of the video games we played at Daniel's.

This hatchet method was taking too long. The hole at shoulder-height was only wide enough for a fist. Better to smash the lock. I struck sideways so that the blade hit at a right angle to the wood. Once, twice, the steel of the hatchet collided with the metal. It became twisted. Wood splintered everywhere. One more hard swing should do it. I was sweating; dust coated the roof of my mouth. Just one more time, I thought. I hit it hard and the lock broke away. But I didn't stop. I wasn't finished yet. I dashed the hatchet against the wood again and again, as if punishing the door for its resistance. By the time I quit, the wardrobe was littered with holes, and the lighter wood from inside spilled out from the piece of furniture like entrails.

Eric grabbed hold of my arm and said, "That's enough. You can stop now; the door's open."

Panting, I let the ax fall.

I felt a little light headed. I wasn't a legal expert, but I knew by breaking open the wardrobe we had crossed another line. We'd begun with trespassing and now we were moving on to property damage. And for what? All we could see was fabric. Neatly folded bedsheets sorted onto different shelves: pillowcases, fitted sheets, blankets with old-fashioned patterns—tiny flowers, gingham, more tiny flowers. It smelled like mildew and lavender and mold.

Schulz tore the linens off the shelves and shook them out in the hope that bills would be hidden somewhere inside them. Sam—and here we probably should've noticed that something wasn't quite right—started picking up the discarded sheets, folding them, and laying them neatly in a pile. For the first time, I realized the chaos that we were creating. Leaning against the wall was the cut-up mattress with the chef's knife sticking out of it. The slats of the bed frame had been broken, and next to it lay the scattered contents of the nightstand drawer: knick-knacks, slips of paper, costume jewelry. In front of the bedroom door a mountain of fabric was steadily piling up, and Schulz was still trying to add to it. Everything was littered with wood splinters. The ax lay in the corner. Dust swirled through the air. We were all panting. Meanwhile, outside the house, the sun shone, sparrows twittered, and in a house nearby, some lady was probably ironing clothes for her husband, who would be mowing the grass on the weekend.

"Cut it out!" said Eric. "Stop. Leave it. Leave it alone. We're not finding anything."

We all looked at him. Sam let go of a blanket with a purple blossom pattern.

Eric didn't say anything. Instead, he went back to the doorway, where the chair was lying after Schulz had pushed it away. He brought it back and placed it in front of the wardrobe. The seat, sheathed in a piece of plastic wrap, was smeared with grease and covered with leftover food. Eric wiped his sticky fingers on his pants, then got on the chair. He reached into the highest shelf of the wardrobe, which

PHILIPP MATTHEIS

was smaller than all the others. He peered inside and turned toward us, grinning. He seemed about to say something, but the only sound that came out was a chortle. He produced a plastic bag with something in it. There *had* to be something in it, right?

Eric got down from the chair. The bag was about the size of a lady's pocketbook and it sagged. We waited for him to open it. But Eric wrapped the bag in his arms, looked at us briefly—and just walked out of the room.

Sam pulled his bandanna down from his mouth. "Eric! W-wait!"

Eric went into the kitchen, and we followed. Then he did something really bizarre. He took one of the mildewed cookies deteriorating in a package on the table, placed it on his outstretched hand, and said, "Whoever eats this can have what's in the bag."

"What the fuck?" I demanded. "Just open it!"

Eric pretended not to hear me. "Whoever wants what's inside has to eat the cookie." He held it up for us to see. The cookie was half covered in green, furry mold.

"So . . . Who's it gonna be?"

No one said anything.

"G-give us the b-bag! It's not funny."

"You want me to give you the bag? I'll give it to you. No problem. I'm happy to. But first, you eat the cookie."

"G-g-give us the bag," Sam said again. I murmured my agreement. Schulz said nothing.

"No problem, Sam. You can have the bag. But first, you have to eat the cookie."

"N-no."

What had gotten into Eric? This was unbelievable. Sam's eyes got bigger and bigger, looking from the bag to the cookie and back again.

"Okay, Sam. Let's make a deal: You can have half of what's in the bag, and you don't have to eat the whole cookie. You just have to take one bite. How about that? That's a damn good bargain: one bite of a moldy cookie for half of what's in this bag. Of course, I can't tell you what's inside. Maybe it's not money. Maybe it's just," he took a peek into the bag, "maybe there's just a bunch of granny panties. Or maybe not . . . What do you think?"

Sam gazed at him like a dancing snake hypnotized by a flute player.

Suddenly, a hand snatched for the bag. It was Schulz. "Damn it, you asshole, give us the bag!"

Eric was not only faster than Schulz, he was also taller and stronger. In a split second his arm raised the bag higher than Schulz could reach. With his other hand he grabbed Schulz by his shirt collar. Schulz tried to retreat.

"What?" Eric demanded, his voice deep and challenging. "What? What is it? Hmm? What do you want?"

"Eric, let him go," I pleaded.

He looked at me. Then he actually did let Schulz go. Schulz slumped down and left the room.

"It's a fair deal that me and Sam are making, right?" Eric winked at me, as if this was just a joke, as if making Sam eat the cookie would be something we'd laugh ourselves to death about years later.

"Eric, that's enough. It's not funny anymore. Just leave him alone."

But Eric ignored me. He turned back to Sam, who, for whatever reason, hadn't moved the whole time. Eric, who had dropped his cookie when he grabbed Schulz, now took another, equally moldy cookie from the package and held it in front of Sam's nose while brandishing the plastic bag in the air.

He said, "Come on, one bite, and you'll get half."

He winked at me again over Sam's shoulder, as if we were allies in this fucked-up game. And actually—I couldn't help but grin back, even though I didn't think it was funny at all.

"Just one bite."

Sam reached for the cookie. He didn't say a word. Eric let Sam take it, gingerly and solemnly, as if this were a ceremony. Now the furry cookie lay in Sam's hand, and he slowly bent his head toward it to sniff it.

Suddenly, Schulz returned to the kitchen holding the ax in his hand, still wearing his sunglasses. He looked like the Terminator.

"You fucking faggot!" he shouted. "Give us the bag!"

Sam dropped the cookie, and Eric retreated two steps. Schulz brought the ax down so it split the air between me and Sam and hit the plywood of the graying kitchen table with a thunderous roar.

"We do this together, got it?" Schulz growled. "We came in together, and we split everything we find here. Got it?"

Eric, his back to the kitchen window, hesitated a second while he swallowed his fear. Then he grinned mischievously.

"Schulz, get a grip. Chill out. It was just a joke, okay? Obviously we're gonna split it. What kind of person do you think I am? You really think I'd let any of you guys take all of it?"

Schulz didn't let go of the ax until Eric placed the plastic bag on the kitchen table and opened it for all of us to see.

Then Eric reached into the bag and began pulling out bills, dividing them one after another into four piles. We stared spellbound at the steadily rising stacks.

Ten long minutes later, we took our piles of 150 hundred-mark bills and shoved the cash into whatever empty pockets we could find.

ELEVEN

Before we left the house, Sam did another strange thing. We were in the empty room—the one next to the patio. Schulz had one foot out the door when Sam suddenly said, "Wait a sec," and then he turned and ran down the basement stairs.

We had no idea what he was up to. Sam never struck out on his own; usually he did what everyone else was doing. While we waited, we started smoking. No one said anything. Eric inhaled on his cigarette with so much force that its ember expanded to a full inch. The corners of his lips lifted up into a self-satisfied smile. Schulz shifted uneasily from foot to foot. I really just wanted to get out of there. I felt my pockets. They were so stuffed I was afraid that something might fall out while I was walking. I pushed the money and letters farther down, pulled my hoodie over my head, and asked what everyone else wanted to do now. "Wanna get drunk?" I suggested. No one responded.

We continued smoking in silence—everyone looking in a different direction—until Sam came back. He looked confused and stumbled across the room, trying unsuccessfully to regain his composure. He was bent over like a hunchback, and little beads of sweat shone on his forehead.

"What'd you want from downstairs?" Eric asked.

Sam didn't answer. He just passed right by us and went outside. When he saw that we didn't immediately follow but were just standing there finishing our cigarettes, he turned around, stuck his head back in, and hissed, "W-w-what are you waiting for? Let's go! Let's *go*! *Come on*!"

We put out our cigarettes on the concrete of the patio and left. *For the last time*, I thought to myself. We trudged across the lawn, with the dandelions leaving milky sap spots on our pant legs. We exited through the break in the hedge and were back in the open. We hurried down Flower Street, not looking around, not saying a word to one another. Schulz ran ahead. He hadn't once taken his sunglasses off. Sam, sweating, followed him. I ran behind Eric and tried to keep pace with his commanding strides.

We turned the corner where Flower Street curved, and suddenly this woman was standing there with her dog who stared at us with its black dog eyes and its searching, striving nose. The woman was about sixty years old and dressed in a blue-and-red-checked smock, like something a cleaning lady would wear. She stopped to examine us. The dog was actually pretty small, a dachshund or something, and it and the woman seemed to sniff at us in the same way, but maybe that was just my imagination.

We moved past her one by one: Schulz first, hiding behind his sunglasses; then me; then Sam, obscured beneath his baseball cap; and finally Eric, who hung back and looked the woman straight in the eyes, almost confrontationally. The dog barked, and she pulled on the leash and dragged the dog close to her. I turned back and saw that she had also turned to look at us. I felt paralyzed. By the time I realized I'd stopped, Eric and the others were already a good fifty feet ahead of me. I sprinted to catch up to them and fell in with Sam. He was looking at the ground. I asked him if everything was okay, but he didn't answer. He just went faster, as if he hadn't heard me. We turned onto Main Street and the noise of the cars was somehow calming. They sounded normal—not like the eerie silence of the yard and the house. The sun was shining, too. Farther down I could see the yellow walls of the supermarket. That's where we were headed. I couldn't help reaching into my pockets to feel the reassuring paper.

We entered the supermarket parking lot—a monotonous panel of asphalt about as big as a football field—and Eric told us to hold up. The perimeter was lined with little knee-high bushes. But Sam wasn't watching and his hat was pulled down almost over his eyes, so he walked right into them. He managed to pull his left hand out of his pocket to try to catch himself, but he still fell face down on the asphalt. He lay on the ground, his hat beside him, and swore. Eric laughed and Schulz helped him up.

"You okay?" Schulz asked.

Sam reached for his hat and put it back on, adjusting it. Then he felt his pockets and, finding the bundles, looked satisfied. His small, dark eyes peered at Schulz as if he had just woken him up from a nap.

"So . . ." Eric said, as if he were getting ready to make an announcement. He straightened up, posing like a military commander. He looked pretty stupid, but I have to admit that it worked. We waited for whatever he was going to say. Behind him a shopping cart clattered over the asphalt, heading toward a red station wagon.

"What now?" asked Schulz.

Eric looked slightly annoyed to be interrupted. The cart kept clattering.

Finally, Eric said, "I've got to say good-bye to you."

"What?"

"I'm gonna disappear for a while. I can't tell you any details. It would be too dangerous. But hey, it's been awesome. We had a lot of fun. But look, I'm sorry about before. I have a plan. Everyone has their own destiny that they have to follow. I've found mine and I have to follow it. I'm from the ghetto, and in the ghetto there's only two possibilities: You're either a gangster or a loser. And I've made my decision. You guys get it. Of course you get it. Maybe we'll see each other again, maybe not. It is what it is. Actually, I'm sure we'll see each other again. And then, then . . . Well, I don't want to say too much. But it's gonna be awesome. Really awesome. No more bullshit. I just can't talk about it now. It wouldn't be professional, and I gotta be careful."

One at a time, he took a step toward each of us, said our name, and shook our hand. We didn't say anything. We were completely dumbstruck.

Just before he turned to go, Eric said to me, "Don't forget to read *Chariots of the Gods*, okay?"

Then he put his big headphones over his ears, gave a little whistle, and trudged off toward the train station. Seeing him walk away, I thought he looked like a hobo.

"He's nuts," said Schulz. "What was all that ghetto bullshit?"

"G-g-ghetto gangster bullshit," repeated Sam. At least he was talking again.

"Yesterday he was going on and on about Zafko and getting into the business," I said.

Schulz pushed his Ray-Bans up over his black hair. His eye looked like shit.

"He's crazy. What a dumbass," he said.

I said that we should go inside because I wanted to get something to drink. "Also, I kinda want to steal something," I said.

"What are you, stupid?" Schulz shot back. "We don't have to steal anything anymore. We'll never have to steal anything ever again. From now on we're only gonna *buy* stuff. And we're gonna buy everything! Booze, clothes, candy, PlayStation games, cars, girls." He gave a short laugh: "Everything, we're just gonna buy everything!"

He was right, in a way, but what I'd learned was that buying something just isn't as exciting as stealing it.

We should have gotten a shopping cart, but we didn't bother. We just went through the brightly colored aisles and grabbed anything that was even vaguely appealing, stuffed it under our arms, and went to the register. On the conveyer belt we put a six-pack of Heineken, a lineup of mini Jack Daniels bottles, six packs of cigarettes (red Winstons, Marlboro Lights, and, for Schulz, two packs of Davidoffs at eight marks a pack), Twinkies, gummy bears, Cheetos, Funyuns, gum, and a *Playboy*.

"I'll pay," Schulz said and pulled a bill out of his pocket. The register opened and the bill was placed with the other hundred-mark bills, secured with a plastic lever, and exchanged for some cleaner bills. Sam took the wad of cash and coins and stuffed it all in the sagging pocket of his baggy pants. Then we went to the half-pipe.

"D-d-does anyone have anything to smoke?" Sam asked as he pulled a Heineken out of the cardboard container. The cap flew off and tumbled through the air, landing with a muted clink on the blacktop.

We shook our heads. Now that Eric was gone, we didn't really know what to do anymore. We'd lost our compass.

"Dan might have something," I said.

"Does he sell?" asked Schulz.

"Not really. He always says he doesn't want to deal. But maybe we can make him an offer he can't refuse."

Schulz giggled like a little kid. Our bottles clinked as we tapped them together. Some beer sloshed over my hand. We lay flat on our backs on the asphalt. Around us were cigarette packs, bottles of Jack Daniels, and all the rest of our stuff. We smoked our cigarettes while still on our backs, sitting up only to take a swig of beer.

"I've got a French test tomorrow," I said. I had to laugh. Schulz snorted.

"What a load of shit."

I said, "I don't think I'm gonna go to school. I'm gonna skip and we can go to the city. Or just get drunk."

At that moment I felt a burden fall away from me. It was like that sensation I'd had in the McDonald's, only more complete. I think maybe what I was feeling was a sense of real freedom. Other people who had cooler clothes, who got better grades, who could skate better, or who had Jeep Wranglers—I really didn't care about them anymore. We were friends and we had money. Things were really getting started now.

"Do you think he'll come back?" I asked.

"I don't care," said Schulz.

"H-he's got nothing now. No school, no home, no nothing."

"Why don't you cry about it," said Schulz. "It's his own fault. I think he'll be back soon. He'll run out of money faster than he thinks. Then he'll come and beg us for some. Just wait and see."

"Jack Daniels," said Sam, sitting up and reaching for the array of little bottles in front of him. He threw one to me and one to Schulz, and they landed on our stomachs.

"So, Sam. What were you doing in the basement?" asked Schulz.

"B-b-basement?"

"Yeah, why did you even go down there? And why were you acting so weird afterward?"

"W-w-weird?"

"Yeah, w-w-weird. Stop repeating everything I say."

Sam looked quickly to the right and then to the left, like he was checking for eavesdroppers. Then he lowered his head toward us and whispered:

"B-b-bones!"

"B-b-bones?" echoed Schulz.

"B-b-bones!"

"B-b-bones."

"C-can you stop repeating everything?" I said. "What kind of bones? Chicken bones? Dog bones? Human bones? What kind of bones were they?"

Sam took another Jack Daniels, twisted the top off, and chugged the whole thing.

"Just b-b-bones. There were b-b-bones. I dug deep down into the mound of dirt. Wanted to see what was in it. With the sh-sh-shovel. I was digging and then s-s-suddenly there were b-b-bones."

Sam's stuttering could be so irritating sometimes.

"But you didn't have a flashlight. How did you manage to see anything?" Schulz said.

Sam looked at him questioningly.

"Chill out. You just imagined it. It was way too dark to be able to see any 'b-b-bones.'" Schulz stood up and rubbed Sam's shoulder, as if he were a dog that needed petting. "Maybe you s-s-smoke too much weed."

"S-s-stop m-making fun of me all the time. If you had a st-st-st-stu-, st-stutter, it . . ." he swallowed the next few words, ". . . so funny."

TWELVE

I drank a quart of milk. Fresh, white, sweet milk. Then I got into bed and pulled the covers up to my chin. I was exhausted, but there was an anxiety in my fatigue that kept me from falling asleep. After tossing and turning for half an hour, thinking about the money, the house, Eric, and the bones—everything that had happened that day—I flipped on the TV and smoked a cigarette. It felt like everything was pulling me under, trying to suck me down into a gigantic wave and spit me out in some remote corner of the universe.

I put the TV on mute, like Sam always did when he was trying to fall asleep. He'd learned this from a stoner who used to sell him overpriced weed. The guy told him that the silent images stimulated your brain while you slept and opened doors to your unconscious or something. I thought about that stoner. He'd always reminded me of a mole. I watched the TV news guy talking, unable to hear a word. I thought how cool it would be if whenever someone got annoying you could just turn off the sound. If there were a mute button for teachers, parents, security guards, and all the other assholes. It would also be pretty damn funny. When you couldn't hear what he was saying, the news guy went from looking really serious to looking really hilarious. That was exactly what made Sam so cool, that he didn't talk much.

In my desk drawer was over fifteen thousand marks, and Eric was on his way to . . . Where was he going? What was that weird mobster farewell speech all about? And what had he actually said? He'd been talking a lot about Zafko and comm and P's. He wanted to be a dealer, and he really meant it.

And what was up with Sam? He couldn't have seen any bones down in the basement. This was reality, after all, not a horror movie. I wished I had someone to talk to, like a friend who was normal, or a girlfriend. I thought of Lena. Eventually I fell asleep still thinking about her.

❛ ❜ ❟

The next day, after school, I set out for the half-pipe alone. I hadn't seen Sam, Eric was gone, and Schulz, as usual, had other plans. I didn't mind. I took my skateboard with me so I could practice some tricks by myself, without smoking any weed or drinking anything. I had a few bills in my pocket, but I'd left the rest in my desk drawer. I didn't really feel comfortable leaving all that money there, though, and planned to find somewhere better soon.

I passed through the chilly underground walkway at the train station. On the way I scanned the tags on the wall tiles. Most of the graffiti was just dicks and pussies. Up above I could hear the train stopping. Within seconds, people began streaming down the steps. Then, amid the crush of bodies, briefcases, and newly lit cigarettes, I saw her. She was coming down the stairs, and in two seconds we would run right into each other. Seeing her made me lose my train of thought. I became scared that I wouldn't have anything interesting, or at least coherent, to say. She was wearing a short black dress with spaghetti straps. Her hair spilled over her shoulders in waves, and she looked as cool as ice behind a pair of dark sunglasses. Meanwhile, I was wearing pants that were two sizes too big and a bright blue T-shirt. I was still a boy, and she was practically a woman. She looked like one, anyway. I tried to smile like I knew something she didn't, partly because I thought that was something that worked for me, but also because I didn't know what else to do. She seemed not to see me. Maybe it was too dark with those sunglasses on. She walked past me.

"Lena!" I called.

She turned back toward me, slowly, lazily. I was suddenly aware of the sound of all the wooden soles and high-heeled shoes clacking against the concrete.

"Oh. Heyyy Jonnn." The creaky way she said it made it sound like she'd just woken up. It was like she didn't even care enough to say my name. It sounded stupid.

"Where are you headed?"

"To see Schulziiiie." She drew out the last syllable in another winding creak.

"Oh yeah?" I asked, still smiling, but looking more nervous than cool, I was sure.

"Yeah, where else? What about yooou?"

"Skating," I answered. "I'm going skating."

"It's so cute how you still like doing that. Have fun with all the twelve-year-olds, I guess. I've gotta run. I'm already late. See ya."

Then she walked away. I watched her go. The hem of her dress swayed back and forth as she went. I was frozen in place, and I kept standing there after all the commuters had disappeared.

What was that all about? What had changed? I mean, it was only two days ago that we'd talked on the phone about really personal stuff, about the house, Schulz, the money. And now? I turned over my skateboard and looked at the bottom. When I'd bought it six months ago, there was a picture of a naked woman sprawled out on top of a garbage can. Now, her mud-splattered upper body was scratched up from all the slides.

Have fun with all the twelve-year-olds. Twelve-year-olds, my ass. She sounded like the pseudo-intellectual girls in my class who were always reading Virginia Woolf and dating older guys with cars. I trudged up the steps and threw my board onto the asphalt. I reached into my pocket and pulled out a bill. The sun was shining; people were coming and going from the stores and the train station. I took the bill and held it up with both hands so that it just covered the sun. On it, an old man in a black beret peered out from his blue, two-dimensional world. At that moment there was a gust of wind, and I let go. The bill flew up, turned on its own axis, dropped a little, and then was lifted up again. It sailed slowly to the ground. I watched it settle on the asphalt. None of the people walking by even noticed the money. I jumped onto my board and rolled down the narrow path to the half-pipe.

When I got there, Schulz was waiting for me, purple eye and all. "Hey," he said.

"What are you doing here?"

"Just hanging out. Waiting for whoever showed up."

"It's just weird to see you out of bed while the sun is up. And anyway . . . I thought Lena was at your place."

"Nope, not today. Something's changed. I don't see the point of just lying around anymore. Lately I feel really"— he balled his hand into a fist—"full of energy. You know? There's finally something happening."

"Are things with Lena okay?"

"Oh yeah. She's not mad about the money anymore. I actually think she's kind of excited about it. She just doesn't want to admit it. I mean, you know how she used to be all crazy about that guy Thomas and his Wrangler? She's really into stuff like that."

"But you don't have your license and it'll be forever until you get it."

"Yeah. But who says I need a license to drive a car?"

"Where are you gonna get a car? Who do you think is gonna sell you one?"

"Who says it'll be legal? I'm not sure how yet, but I'll figure it out. It'll work. Can't you just see the look on Lena's face when I show up at her place in a car? She won't care where it came from then."

I shrugged and got on my skateboard. I was too exhausted to try any tricks, so I just rode up and down the mini ramp. Schulz didn't make any move to get up. He lit himself a cigarette.

"Eric's a pretentious asshole," he said, after puffing a few smoke clouds into the sun.

"He wasn't trying to show off, I don't think. He just sounded kind of crazy. I think he's been watching too many movies."

"He thinks he's some kind of gangster. He thinks he can act like some kind of drug lord and everyone's gonna respect him."

I rolled up, I rolled down.

"Come on, you know he didn't mean it like that. Don't hold it against him. He always exaggerates. You shouldn't take him so seriously all the time."

"Why don't we go to Munich this weekend, to Terminal? I'm ready to spend some cash," he said.

"Because they wouldn't let us in.

"We can bribe the bouncers. We'll slip each of them a bill and then we're in. Come on, live a little. We could get LSD there, or coke. You want to try and do some coke?"

THIRTEEN

It was like Sam had been in a trance for the entire taxi ride. His eyes scanned the guardrails flashing by, moving from left to right and then jumping back again, over and over again. It was like he was reading some amazing line in a book that only he could understand. When he finally broke free from his hypnosis, he started to hum "Some-where over the Rainbow." His humming was so loud that you could easily hear it over the sound of the engine.

I peered between the two front seats, trying to catch a glimpse of the meter. The price didn't worry me; I was just fascinated by the fact that we could now afford some-thing that was once so utterly extravagant. I couldn't see the fare, though; the driver's hand was blocking the digits. The car slowed as we got off the expressway. In front of us was my first landmark, the high-rise. I didn't know who owned the building or what it was used for, but for me that was the place where the city started. It was beige, with black windows alternating with sections of white wall on the front. It looked like an enormous piano rammed sideways into the ground. The driver turned right.

"Wait, where are we supposed to find him?" I asked.

"In the park."

"Sam, the park is huge! Didn't he tell you where to go? You talked on the phone. The . . ."

"E-Eric said somewhere near the Monopoly."

"What the hell . . ." I saw the driver's eyes in the rearview mirror and lowered my voice. "What the hell does that mean, 'somewhere near the Monopoly'?"

"It's a hill or something. I couldn't really make out what he was saying, but it sounded like Mo-Mo-Monopoly or Monopolis. Sounded Latin or something." He gave a shrug and said, "W-w-what do I know?"

We were driving past a monument. On the other side, the surface of the river rippled with reflections of the sky and the chestnut trees. For a minute I imagined what it would be like to jump into the river and let myself be carried away, all the way to the sea. We could easily live off the money for a year or two—anywhere in the world. We could buy a house, maybe on a beach in the Caribbean or in Asia. Eric could build his business, and we could all work for him. Later we could invest in the stock market and eventually become millionaires. Sam was now bobbing his head, as if to the beat of a song. But the cab's radio was off and Sam wasn't wearing headphones. Just that stupid, ever-present Yankees baseball hat.

"Why do you keep nodding your head?"

He didn't respond.

"Sam! Why are you nodding your head?"

"W-what?"

"Why are you nodding your head?"

"Dunno."

Sam looked out the window again.

The taxi turned right, then left. It stopped at the park entrance.

"Comes to ninety-two thirty," the driver said.

I pulled a bill out of my pocket, handed it to him, and told him to keep the change.

We grabbed our boards—even though I wasn't really sure why we'd brought them—and got out. Before the taxi drove away, I asked the driver if he knew where the Monopolis was. He just shook his head and took off.

Sam walked straight to the concession stand at the shaded park entrance. He bought eight beers, gave three to me, stowed four in his Eastpak backpack, and opened the last one. The sun elbowed through the leaves of the trees. It was July, and it was hot, but Sam was sweating way more than he should have been. Damp spots on his shirt stretched from his armpits to the bottom of his rib cage. His face shone as if he'd just come out of a sauna. I asked him why he didn't take off his jacket, which had grass stains and dirt on it anyway. Sam said, "Don't feel like it," and took a drink. We crossed the stone bridge over the brook.

Two girls walked toward us. One had shoulder-length dreadlocks and a nose ring. She wore a purple skirt and was taller than Sam and me. The other girl had shaved the left side of her head. I thought she looked about sixteen, but she could have been younger—I wasn't really sure. They were drop-dead gorgeous, mostly because they looked so cool.

I figured the best way to handle it was to just keep walking straight ahead, then maybe nod and say a word or two right as we passed them. Anything more would be too complicated, too risky. But Sam sped up and headed straight toward them. He made me nervous. Sam stopped abruptly in front of the girls and took a drink. I stayed five steps behind him and turned the other way.

"D-d-do you guys know the Monopo-Monopolisaurus?"

The girl with the half-shaved head kept walking, ignoring Sam like she'd already been through this a thousand times before. Her friend with the dreadlocks looked at Sam and—incredibly—smiled. I mean, how often do girls smile when you talk to them? That never happened, at least not at home. Shocked, Sam sucked on his beer like a giant pacifier and wouldn't remove it from his mouth.

"Sorry, what?" the girl asked. Her nose ring glinted in the sun.

I came over and stood next to Sam. Behind the girls was a big green expanse, and about a hundred yards away was a hill with a little gazebo on top. The sun poured over everything. There wasn't a cloud in sight.

Sam moved his bottle an inch away from his mouth, which made it look like he was about to blow across the top to make a foghorn noise.

"Mono-, Molo, Monolopol, or something. A hill or something, with s-some sort of c-columns, La-Latin or something."

The girl laughed, but she was laughing with him, not at him: She actually thought he was funny. I could hardly believe it. She was a half a head taller than him.

"You mean the Monopteros. It's up there."

She turned and pointed to the hill with the gazebo.

"You guys aren't from around here," her friend said.

"Nope," Sam answered, and I silently thanked the summer, the city, and everything else for what he said next. "We're from B-Berlin. We're here on a school trip."

"You're from Berlin?" asked the one with the half-shaved head.

"Yeah, Berlin," I repeated.

"Wow, what's it like?" asked the tall one.

"Pretty cool," said Sam.

"Yeah, Berlin's cool," I said.

"Cool."

"So . . . you're from here then," I guessed.

"Yeah," she answered.

"Well, there's the Monopteros," she said, and then they started walking away. "Maybe we'll see you later. We were gonna stop by there tonight."

"Cool. Drinks, drugs . . . everything's on us!" Sam said to their backs.

Luckily, they were already too far away and didn't seem to hear him. Sam had meant it in the nicest way possible, but it definitely sounded creepy.

Without saying another word, we scurried up toward the hill. Off to the left we heard drumming; here and there birds twittered, and pebbles crunched under the rubber soles of our shoes. The air smelled like sunscreen, cigarette smoke, and freshly mown grass. Sam pulled his sunglasses from his jacket pocket. Once they were on, only the lower half of his face was still visible.

"Ray-Bans," he said.

"Pretty smooth there, playa," I said.

He just smiled. For the first time in pretty much ever, Sam seemed genuinely confident and self-assured.

Once we reached a spot where the hill began to steepen, we took a seat under a small tree. Sam opened a second beer; I opened my first. The drumming was louder, and a tangle of voices floated down to us from the gazebo. On the horizon we could see the towers of a church against the sky. Sam cleared his throat.

"When's Eric coming?" I asked.

"I don't know. He said he was coming, though. Whenever he gets here, I guess."

"Yeah, okay, whatever." I fell back into the grass and tried to relax.

•   •   •

It was getting dark. The sun was sinking behind the towers of the church and the South American drumming continued in the warm evening air—unstoppable, as if someone had wound it like a clock. Sam had been napping for about an hour. I made a few attempts at conversation, but he just grunted. I'd drunk the three beers in my bag and was feeling a little wobbly.

In the distance I saw someone with a familiar walk, broad and elastic and almost celebratory, except for the duffel bag slung over his shoulder—which forced Eric to bend forward slightly. He was wearing navy blue baggy pants, a green short-sleeved shirt, and a baseball cap turned backward. I shook Sam to wake him. Sam sat up, waved, and shouted Eric's name. But Eric didn't walk any faster, as if it were beneath his dignity to speed up. His pace remained steadily determined.

"Sam," said Eric when he reached us. He held out his hand. Sam launched into a stuttering flurry of questions, but Eric turned away, looked to me, and held out his hand as he said my name.

He dropped his duffel bag and sat next to us in the gradually dampening grass. He spotted the beer, opened one of them with his lighter, and downed a quarter of it in one gulp.

"Where have you been since the last time we saw you?" I asked.

Before answering, he looked toward the evening sun, now sunk behind the church tower, and lit a cigarette.

Then he grinned, puffed, and blew the smoke up into the cloudless sky.

"Here. I've been here."

FOURTEEN

All Eric had in his duffel bag was a hoodie, two T-shirts, some dirty clothes, a bong, and a plastic bag of weed. Eric glanced furtively over his shoulder before pulling out the enormous bag. Sam and I had never seen so much weed in one place before. I opened it up and the smell was almost overpowering. I reached in and ran my fingers over the bounty. Resin stuck to my fingertips. I tasted it and gave the bag to Sam. It was bitter.

"That's insane. How much do you have?"

"Guess!" said Eric.

"A p-p-pound?"

"You retard!" said Eric. "Do you know how much a pound weighs?"

Sam shrugged his shoulders.

"A pound is way more! That's half a pound."

"Half a p-pound? Jesus."

Eric pulled some rolling papers out of his pocket and started to work on a joint.

"We can't smoke a bong out here," he said. "It's too obvious. I have to be more careful now that I'm in the business." He wasn't rolling the joint in the normal way. Instead he did this awsome thing that I'd never seen anyone else do; he rolled the joint backward and licked the paper inside out. Then he burned off the extra paper, so that he made a joint using only a single layer.

The sun had set, leaving only a pale, reddish glow. Someone was still pounding on the bongo across the hill.

So Eric had been serious. He told us how he'd gone to Zafko, spread his cash out on the table, and requested half a pound.

"You shoulda seen his face when I showed him the money," he said, turning the tip of the joint carefully in the flame of his lighter.

But apparently, Zafko had tried to rip him off after that. He'd disappeared for a minute into the kitchen and returned with a plastic bag full of weed.

"The faggot tried to give me a QP. He said that was all he had."

And the price had suddenly gone up from what they'd agreed on: Instead of one pound for three thousand marks, now it was half a pound for eighteen hundred.

"But it's okay," said Eric. "I'm gonna make twenty-two hundred from that eighteen. Not bad for a beginner. All I've gotta do is sell each gram for ten marks."

He puffed a cloud of smoke into the air and handed me the joint. The past few days he'd been wandering through the park asking people who looked like potential customers whether they wanted to buy any weed.

"How much have you sold?" I asked.

He took a drink.

"Well, I'm just getting started, but over the past two days I've gotten rid of about a quad."

"A quad? A quarter ounce?! If it takes you two days to sell a quad, it's gonna take months before you can empty the bag."

"That's some shit math. I know I've still got a ways to go. There's a learning curve, and anyway I'm just getting started. Any business takes a little time to really get going. Anyway, at least it's a plan. You always talk shit about everything." His voice thudded in my ears as I studied the ground. He took another drink, inhaled, and then breathed out slowly.

"It'll work," he said, more quietly. "It'll be fine."

"You're fucking crazy!" Sam shouted. Eric and I were totally shocked. Sam reached over and grabbed the joint from my fingers.

"Chill out," I told him. It was dark, but Sam was still wearing his sunglasses. He sucked on the joint like it was an inhaler—like he needed it to survive.

He said, "Shut up," and began to bob his head again to a rhythm only he could hear.

"Eric," I said, "we're going to Terminal on Friday. Schulz is organizing it. You should come."

Eric nodded; he didn't seem very interested. He told us about the people he'd met in the park over the last few days. One of them was a guy named Joe. "He's got crooked teeth and he's short," said Eric. "Looks like a rat and always talks about how he's got gypsy blood in him. He says he's a thief. But he's a funny guy, hits on like every girl that walks by."

Apparently Joe still owed Eric thirty marks for three grams of weed. He'd promised to give it to him the next time they ran into each other. Joe told Eric that he was never far from the park. But that was yesterday afternoon, and Eric hadn't seen him again since. There was someone else who everyone called Coconut or just Coco. I asked Eric if he always walked around with a coconut or something. "No," Eric replied. "One time he just took too much LSD and never came back down again. Now he's convinced that he's a coconut. But still, he's really cool." Eric had also sold weed to a couple of skinheads. And in the mornings, around sunrise, there were always a few people coming from Terminal, still high out of their minds, who sat in the park to smoke a joint and come down. "There's some really messed up shit that happens here," said Eric.

Eric packed up his duffel bag and stood up.

"Let's go up to the top," he said. We got up with him.

A paved walkway wound around and led to the gazebo. Just past the first bend, some sort of Goa trance music rattled out of a stereo. Sam bobbed his head faster. The stereo gradually overwhelmed the sounds of the few remaining bongo drummers. After the second bend, I lit a cigarette.

When we finally got to the top, we saw about fifteen people sitting in the gazebo. Candles were set up everywhere.

The two girls we'd met on the bridge were already there. The hippie girl with dreadlocks was smoking weed out of a pipe (improvised from a plastic Coke bottle). The girl with the half-shaved head was wrapped in a purple shawl. A big batik cloth was spread out in front of them. A wiry guy covered in tattoos danced around. He'd taken his shirt off and his head was shaved bald except for a tuft at the back, which was gathered into a high ponytail. "That's Coconut," said Eric.

"Look, those guys from Berlin are here," said the girl with the dreadlocks, waving.

"*Guys from Berlin?*" Eric repeated.

"Me and Sam told them we're from Berlin," I whispered to him.

We sat down and introduced ourselves. The girl with the dreads was named Susie and her friend was Julia. Julia ignored us and looked in the opposite direction.

"Jules is having a bad day," Susie said. "Her parents are giving her crap about school and stuff. But we'll be gone soon."

"G-gone?" asked Sam. It was the first word that had come out of his mouth since he'd told me to shut up.

"We're going to India soon. Right, Jules?"

She nudged her friend, who nodded.

"Berlin would be cool, too. Where do you guys live?"

Coconut's arm swooshed over my head as he danced, shirtless. His entire upper body was almost completely covered in random Chinese characters and demonic faces. Honestly, I was a little uncomfortable with him dancing so close to us, but I didn't say anything.

"What do you mean? Like where in Berlin?" I asked.

"Yeah, what neighborhood. Kreuzberg?"

"K-Kreuzberg," said Sam.

"Kreuzberg," I repeated.

"Yeah, Kreuzberg," said Eric.

"I think Kreuzberg's awesome! It must be incredibly boring for you here. Munich is so ghetto."

"Fuck Munich, and fuck the police state," said Julia.

Eric asked them what they were going to do in India. Susie said her dad was kind of a hippie and lived there with a bunch of other hippies in a house on the beach. That question got her going, and all of a sudden she was talking a mile a minute. In fact, she spoke so fast that I only caught a few words: "ocean," "Ganesha," "Gandhi," and "Goa" stood out. At some point Susie paused to reflect and said, "The people there don't have anything, but they're still happy!"

"Is it cheap to live in India?" Eric asked.

"Oh, it's crazy cheap. You can live like a king on like ten marks a day!"

"Seriously?!"

"Yeah, absolutely! It's like being a millionaire there."

Coconut's foot landed on my finger. I jumped up and glared at him, expecting at least an apologetic wave of his hand. But he was already twirling somewhere else. Then Eric took some weed out of his bag and put it out for everyone to help themselves. We were definitely a welcome addition to the group then. Susie was now talking about Indian gods and goddesses, and Eric and Sam kept nodding like they were interested. But that was all Sam did now, nod constantly. I moved slightly away from them and sat down on the stone steps in between two candles because Susie and all this pretentious shit about India was starting to get on my nerves.

I leaned against a column and fiddled with the contents of my pockets. It was a habit now. I liked the feeling of the coarse wad of bills. Then I remembered what else I had on me—the letters from our last break-in. I hadn't trusted myself to look at them yet. So now, under the clear night sky, I took the letters out and looked them over. There were only two envelopes, both folded and creased, and actually kind of gross and sticky. One of them had the brown outline of a coffee mug. I opened it. Unlike the first letter, it wasn't written on a typewriter, and the handwriting was so shaky that it took me awhile to decipher it.

Dear Mr. Mueller,

Something has to be done. This is war. Gertrude's nerves cannot take any more. She shakes like a leaf. The doctor says it's because of the cancer. But I know the truth: I saw the Schneider woman and the rest of them yesterday, sneaking around in front of our yard. She was carrying a bottle with a skull and crossbones on it. Mr. Mueller, you must believe us! Our groceries have been poisoned. They have poisoned our food! I saw them, saw how they weaseled their way into our house so they could sneak the poison into our bread. That's the real reason behind Gertrude's illness, and they are after me, too! They don't want us on this street. They hate us because we're not from here, because we're different. But I will not let them get me. I will not eat their bread, their sick, satanic food. And also, from now on I will boil all our water. It's safer that way. We're safe in the basement, and there's enough room for us down there. But we can't hold out forever. I implore you to help us, Mr. Mueller, before it's too late!

Sincerely,

Hilda Stetlow

Toward the end of the letter, the spiky, angular handwriting became even more jagged so that the last lines were nothing more than scratches. I glanced over my shoulder toward Eric and Sam. Sam, still wearing his sunglasses, was still bobbing his head, but at least he was somewhat in time to the rhythm so his tic wasn't too noticeable. I lit a cigarette and opened the second envelope.

Dear Mr. Mueller,

Why aren't you answering my letters? You're the only person who can help us now! Hate is gaining the upper hand, and we cannot resist it much longer. Gertrude and I have not eaten anything for the last three days. Our groceries have been poisoned. We cannot leave the house. The little devils are lurking out there, and they want to do us harm. Gertrude is doing very poorly; she can only speak in a whisper. She asks for food, but I

*cannot give her any! Mr. Mueller, if Gertrude dies, I will
have no one left. The only thing left will be my hate. If
I need to, I can go into the basement and live off of my
hatred alone. There are tools there . . . with which . . .
must . . . force . . . this hate . . .*

I couldn't make out the last words. At that point, the
writing degenerated into a series of hooked symbols that
looked more like runes than letters. I jumped up and hus-
tled over to Sam and Eric, who were still sitting with Susie
and her friend. When I reached them, I saw Susie take her
hand away from Eric's knee.

"I've got to talk to you," I said, almost shouting
over the music.

"So talk," said Eric.

"Not here . . ."

Muttering, Eric stood up and went with me to the
steps. Sam followed us.

"You guys have to read these!" I said, and I held
the letters out to them. "They're from the house. The
two sisters, they had people after them. Or maybe they
were insane. Or both. It all sounds like some crazy horror movie!"

Eric halfheartedly took one of the letters and scanned
it. He said "cool" and gave it back to me.

Sam said, "I can't read this."

"Maybe you should try taking your damn sunglasses off. What is up with you? Are you retarded or something?"

Sam didn't say anything, but, to my surprise, he took his sunglasses off. He tried to decipher the letters, occasionally saying a word or two out loud. After he'd read the second letter, he put his sunglasses back on and went back to Susie and Julia.

"Someone might have been murdered in that house," I said.

"Sure, why not," said Eric.

"'Sure, why not?' A murder! Don't you get it? This Hilda Stetlow lady might have murdered her sister—or one of the neighbors—and then buried them in the basement!"

The music was really getting annoying.

"Yeah, so what? I honestly don't give a shit about whether someone killed someone else. It all happened a long time ago. It's got nothing to do with us. Actually, what it means is that we shouldn't feel guilty about taking the money. It doesn't matter what we do with it if it just belonged to a couple of crazy old ladies."

"What if the money brings bad luck?" I used Lena's words.

Eric looked right into my eyes, his pupils flashing in the candlelight. At that moment his face reminded me of one of Coconut's tattoos. It was demonic. He gripped my shoulder firmly and said in his heavy, thudding tone, "I don't want to hear any more of this bullshit about bad luck. You watch too many horror movies. You hear me?"

The gazebo had filled up with a whole crowd of hippies, and Coconut was still twirling around on the marble floor behind us. Eric clapped me on the shoulder, and we went back up the steps to Susie and Sam. Sam was sitting Indian-style with his back to us. Something was burning. Suddenly Susie shrieked, "Are you insane? That's more than most Indians make in a whole week! Think of all the starving Indian children!"

Several people looked over to see what was going on.

Sam was burning a handful of bills.

Coconut kept dancing.

FIFTEEN

Schulz shifted his weight back and forth, from one foot to the other. Sometimes he stood on his tiptoes, trying to see over everyone's head to the beginning of the line. Then he sank back down, looked at his new Rolex, and moaned about what a long time it was taking. "What the hell is going on up there . . . The bouncer's an asshole. He gets off on having power, the dick."

He kept his voice was low enough to ensure that the people standing around us couldn't hear. Lena rolled her eyes. Her hair, pulled back into a ponytail, was damp from the rain; a few curly little strands had pulled away from the smoothly brushed top and sides. She looked good. She was dressed pretty casually (which surprised me) in jeans, a black tank top, and a hooded jacket. It was obvious that the cause of her bad mood wasn't standing in line or the rain; it was her boyfriend, Schulz. Schulz ignored this, probably because it was the best way to avoid an outburst. I concentrated on the music pulsating from the building. I couldn't tell what song it was. All I could make out was a muffled, monotonous booming.

Schulz had insisted on coming to Terminal to see some techno DJ I'd never heard of before—despite the fact that he didn't even really like techno. When we'd talked on the phone earlier, he'd promised to get tickets. He also said he was going to talk to some guy that night about buying a car, but it seemed like that wasn't going to work out after all. Not only because Lena was going to be there, but also because he didn't really have the time right now to figure everything out.

Only when we met at the train station two hours before did he admit that he hadn't been able to get tickets. That wouldn't be a problem, he assured us, because we were going to bribe the bouncer anyway. (Which we were already planning to do, since the tickets wouldn't get us very far without ID.) Eric and I didn't care one way or the other. We would have been just as happy getting some Smirnoff Ice and beer and just hanging out and drinking. Ever since Sam's money-burning episode in the park, he'd hardly said a word. He only occasionally responded when he was spoken to, and he often whispered unintelligibly to himself. Sometimes I thought this was creepy, but usually we just laughed about it. Sam seemed to have absolutely no thoughts about where we should go or what we should do. Lena was the only one who cared. She was absolutely set on getting into Terminal to see this DJ. Ever since Schulz admitted, with a guilty look, that he hadn't been able to get tickets, she'd given him the silent treatment.

Only about ten yards and thirty people were between us and the entrance. I could see the red logo was embroidered on the bouncer's brown leather jacket. I'd never bribed anyone before. All I could think of were scenes from random mafia movies where all you see is two hands meeting, and the money changes hands like magic. What if the bouncer didn't play along; what if he didn't take the money? I imagined a situation where the handoff didn't work and the money just floated to the ground, landing on the wet asphalt.

In front of us someone opened an umbrella. I wished I had one. I'd hold it with my left hand, and Lena would squeeze in next to me on my right.

"Hey, anyone want . . . anyone here want weed?"

Eric was asking a group of four men and women behind us if they wanted to buy any weed. They were all wearing orange garbage collector pants, and they all shook their heads. He shrugged.

"I'll just slip three hundreds into his hand," said Schulz. "This dude doesn't earn that much in a week." He laughed his rattling old man laugh.

Eric nodded, grinning, and Lena rolled her eyes again, as if there was no one in the entire world who could possibly annoy her as much as her boyfriend. Two girls greeted the bouncer by kissing him on opposite cheeks. "Have fun," he said, and let them through. Finally, the five of us were standing in front of him, and he was completely serious again. Schulz seemed nervous, alternately pulling stray strands of hair out of his face or shaking his arm so that his gold watch (a replacement) around his wrist was visible. I stuck a ciga-rette in my mouth in an attempt to look a little older. Then I pulled Sam back by the sleeve when, as if remote-controlled, he started to wander off to the side.

"Tickets!" said the bouncer. He sounded like a drill sergeant.

Nothing happened. Everyone waited for Schulz, but he didn't move.

"Let me see your tickets!"

"Uh," said Schulz, and then there was an embarrass-ing silence. Lena turned and stepped away from us, prob-ably trying to make it look like she wasn't in our group. Schulz searched for something in his pocket.

"Tickets, or get out. I don't have all day."

Schulz rummaged uselessly in his pockets while shift-ing from one foot to the other. He turned red. I stepped to the side and stood next to Lena. I could smell the scent of her perfume and caught a glimpse of her bra strap. Sud-denly Eric stepped forward. He spread his body out as wide as possible in front of the bouncer, who was skinny but taller. Eric extended a partially-shielded hand, but the bouncer didn't reach out to meet it.

Five blue bills floated down and landed on top of a wet, dirty grate. As soon as he saw that, the bouncer straight up slapped Eric across the face.

"Fuck off!"

Eric held his cheek. Schulz just watched, literally trembling with fear.

"You think this is the mafia or something? You suburban pricks think you can buy anything with your parents' money. Get out before I call the cops."

Then the bouncer kicked Schulz in the stomach, and Schulz fell backward, down two steps, and onto me and Lena. Lena and I were caught off-guard, and all three of us fell into a puddle. I could hear people shouting behind us, and out of the corner of my eye I saw Eric shove the bouncer. Two more men in matching leather jackets stormed out of the door. Now it wasn't a flat hand landing on Eric's face; it was fists.

"Go home to your parents, you little assholes!" someone yelled. The group wearing the garbage collector pants pushed forward. Lena screamed. One man in a leather jacket punched a skinny guy with blue hair and blue sunglasses. Behind us, someone shouted, "Fucking club Nazis!" and suddenly everyone was pushing and shoving toward the door, as if someone had fired a gun. It became a brawl. I grabbed Lena's arm, but she shrieked at me to let her go. Schulz and Eric were pinned somewhere in the crush of people. Then I saw Sam. He was about fifteen yards away from the crowd and coming straight toward us. In his hands was a three-foot-long metal pole. I ran toward him and rammed my head into his stomach. He swung the pole above me.

"Sam, we're leaving! We're getting out of here!" I shouted.

He snorted. I put all my weight into holding him back. I tried to look him in the eyes—which failed, because he still had his sunglasses on. Lena and Eric joined us. We were outside the brawl, which was in full swing, and finally we were able to calm Sam down and get the pole away from him. We started to run. Tiny drops of rain began to fall, and before long we were sopping wet. We headed toward the subway station. Sweat and rain mixed together. We sat down on the steps of the underground station entrance and smoked cigarettes in the light of the streetlamps.

"Pretty funny, though," said Eric finally, smiling. Sam didn't respond, his sunglass-shielded eyes gazing somewhere toward the street.

"You are totally, utterly insane," said Eric and clapped Sam on the shoulder.

Lena buried her face in her hands. She was muttering about how stupid we all were. Just then I saw a figure limping down the street, dragging his right foot behind. It was Schulz. He sat down between me and Lena and said, "Assholes."

"What happened to your leg?" I asked.

"It's not too bad." He winked at me with his uninjured eye. The other was still bruised from Strasser. Lena didn't even look at him. "I've got more in my pocket than he earns in a month. And he's got a Napoleon complex that he takes out on everyone at the door."

Lena was crying into her hands, but now she looked up. Her face was red.

"You're worse than all of them! You're so fucking stupid, it's embarrassing!"

Schulz, humiliated, didn't say anything. He looked at his watch and wiped the rain from his face.

"What now?" I asked.

"Let's go to Babaloo," said Eric.

"B-B-Babaloo?"

"It's not too far from here. Zafko'll be there tonight."

Lena wiped her tears away and stood up. We walked down to the subway in silence. The platform was empty, except for a few guys who huddled together under the awning. Two of them were delivering kicks to the ticket machine. None of us wanted any more trouble, so we kept a safe distance and stood in the rain. Ten minutes later I saw the flash of the familiar lights. Those two lights, and the empty subway car they were attached to, seemed like the gloomiest thing in the world. But at least the train was going in the right direction.

Sam and I sat across from Eric and Lena. Schulz sat in the row next to us. Sam stared at the raindrops as they dragged themselves down the windowpane. His expression was intense; it seemed like he was deciphering a secret code or something. Now and then he mumbled something to himself and sometimes the gibberish would turn into a really bizarre sort of hissing.

Eric slapped him on the knee. "Dude, what are you babbling about?"

Sam blinked and came back to life, as if he'd been called back from some faraway world. But he still didn't answer. Then he was gone again—focused on the raindrops on the window. Sam wasn't getting on my nerves; he was making me worried. He'd always been weird, but this was too weird. Weird people are also kind of funny, and we laughed about Sam a lot. He was kind of like a pet.

We transferred to another train, rode that one for a few more stops, then got out. The rain had stopped. I took it all in: the puddles reflecting red, yellow, white, and blue, the honking of car horns, the snippets of conversation from people passing by, the tall trees lining the streets, and the brightly lit signs for an ice-cream parlor and a McDonald's.

"They sell syrup around here," said Eric. Syrup, he explained, was slang for codeine, and lots of heroin addicts ended up on it. He knew that from Zafko. Schulz reached for Lena's hand, but she pulled away.

We reached Babaloo. A cluster of people was pressed together in front of the steps, which led downstairs. Everyone looked two or three years older than us, which made the place even more interesting. We forgot about what had happened at Terminal. We had scaled a mountain. We were in the city, and doors that used to be closed to us were now open. We had money.

The bouncer sized us up with a snide look, but once he saw that Lena was with us, he let us in. Eric paid the cover charge for all of us, and a bored-looking girl gave each of us a stamp on the wrist. We went down the steps, past the bathrooms and the coat check. I felt the bass vibrating in my chest. The air was full of steam, sweat, perfume, smoke. It was like a strange skin that covered all of us.

Eric went to the bar and came back with five shots of tequila. He insisted that first we put salt on our hands and lick it off. Just as we were clinking glasses, someone shoved me from behind, and half of my shot spilled over my hand. We drank, then Eric bit into his lemon slice and indicated that we should do the same thing. Without realizing it, we'd arranged ourselves into a little circle. We teetered shyly to the beat—you couldn't really call it dancing. Lena had calmed down. She looked relaxed again, like she was actually having fun. She stuck her tongue out at me. I smiled because I had no idea what that was supposed to mean. She smiled back. I blushed.

For two songs we stood in our circle, then I went to the bar, ordered five Smirnoff Ices, and handed the bartender a fifty. I gestured to him to keep the change. Elbowing my way back to our circle, someone bumped into me again and a Smirnoff Ice splashed over my hand. That annoyed me. I wasn't drunk enough not to care. But if we kept up the pace, then at some point everything would just start happening on its own; I could let the night run its course. Eric pointed at Sam and started to laugh. Probably about his stupid sunglasses. A cigarette was hanging from the corner of his mouth, and he wasn't actually bothering to light it and smoke it. I saw a little smile forming on Lena's lips. And when she looked at me, her smile got bigger. Eric's arm landed forcefully on my shoulder. He bellowed something into my ear, but I couldn't understand him. I could only feel drops of his spit.

"What!?" I shouted back. "I can't hear anything!"

Then he made a motion with his hand that looked something like "fuck it" and went back to the bar. Even here, in a club in the city with hundreds of genuinely cool people, Eric didn't lose any of his self-confidence. He moved through the crowd like he owned the place. I didn't know what to do with my hands, so I went for the simplest option: I lit a cigarette. While Schulz and I shifted stupidly from one foot to the other, and Sam buried his hands in his pockets, Lena was dancing for real. Her whole body was in motion, her hips circling right and left, her arms falling loosely to her sides. With each movement her hair fell into her face, and she was constantly pushing it back behind her ears. She repeated this about every two seconds. Eric came back with five beers. Despite a huge effort, I couldn't make my body move the same way as Lena. After trying for a whole song, I remembered Daniel once said that dancing is for homos. I looked for a wall to lean against and found one. I was glad to find that it was slightly quieter there, too.

Sam stood next to me. "We've gotta watch out. They're f-f-following us."

I started and straightened bolt upright. "Who? The guys from Terminal?" I glanced at the door.

"No, the other ones!"

"Who?" I shouted.

"Th-the . . . w-w-women!"

"What women?"

Instead of answering, he slowly stuck a new cigarette in his mouth. He looked like one of the Blues Brothers. He turned around, and without saying a word, dove back into the dancing crowd.

I put out my cigarette on the floor. Schulz and Lena were shouting in each other's ears while gesturing chaotically. The bathrooms had to be somewhere on the other side of the dance floor. I pushed forward, gently touched shoulders, and moved sideways past all the people, most of whom were a full head taller than me.

Eric was in front of the bathroom talking with someone. The other guy was ugly. Everything about him was puffy. His skin was pale, and red spots were scattered all over his face. His head was shaved on the sides, and the hair on top was totally greased back. He was wearing a Body Count T-shirt. He pretty much looked like a pig. When Eric saw me, he waved me over.

"This is Zafko."

I shook a limp, damp hand.

"What's uuup," said Zafko. The way he stretched it out was probably meant to make him sound chill, but I couldn't hear him over the music. So I said, "Huh?"

"I said, 'What's up,' you ass," barked Zafko.

He turned back to Eric and ignored me. I remembered why I'd come in the first place and went into the bathroom. Everything started spinning. I had to hold myself up on the doorframe.

When I finished pissing, Eric was standing at the sink.

"Zafko's gonna get me some pills, too," he said. "No more weed. Weed's too small time. We're gonna go straight for the big business."

I splashed cold water on my face.

"And then we'll buy a house in the Caribbean," I said randomly.

"Yeah, or in India! You can live like a millionaire down there. We'll buy a house and live on dealing: you, me, Schulz, Lena, Susie, Sam."

"Susie? The India girl?" I asked.

"Yeah, I was actually at her place yesterday."

"What did you do? Anything happen?"

He shook his head.

"No, we just smoked pot. She told me all about Indian religion. It's really interesting. Like, did you know that Ganesha—that's the one with the elephant trunk—Ganesha . . ."

"I don't think Sam's doing so good," I interrupted. "He was just babbling something about women following us."

Eric looked at me in the mirror.

"He's just gotta chill out. I've been telling him that since forever ago."

"But he's acting kind of weird . . ."

"Think about it. We could be in India by fall. Susie told me that her dad lives there, in Goa. We could all live together. We could smoke pot the whole day, eat, and then go for a swim. Once we've earned enough from drugs . . ."

"Maybe we should do something about Sam, like take him to a doctor or something," I said.

"Of course we'll help Sam. We stick together."

He held out his hand for me to shake. Then we hugged.

India . . . , I thought. Eric was right. This India thing really wasn't such a bad idea.

Then I went to the bar and ordered another round of beer, and then another round of Smirnoff Ice. Later I got myself a glass of wine. Sometimes I drank with Eric, sometimes with Sam, and sometimes with some random strangers. And finally, after a while, I stopped thinking altogether. Finally.

SIXTEEN

I cleared my throat again as I pressed the doorbell. Half a minute later she was standing in front of me, in jeans and a white top. "Come in," she told me.

I took off my shoes (the house smelled like fabric softener and cat food) and climbed the carpeted steps in my socks. Her room was pretty big: a pinewood dresser, a small, organized desk, and next to that a little table with a mirror, perfumes, and makeup. There was a small sofa, a TV, and a twin bed covered with a blue satin comforter. I'd never been to Lena's house before.

It was the beginning of August now, school was over, and Lena had called me earlier to ask if I wanted to watch a movie. I'd said yes, of course. I wondered what Schulz would have thought if he knew about it. Then again, watching a movie together wasn't cheating, so how could he really object. We were just friends. And anyway, Lena was the one in a relationship, not me.

I sat on the sofa, and Lena went over to put on the movie. Something was clearly wrong. She pressed at some random buttons, fumbled with plugs and cables, and then swore and sat back down. She laid her hands on her knees.

"It's not working. I don't know how to work a VCR," she said.

I offered to take a look at it. I was actually pretty good with electronics, especially with VCRs, because back when Eric still lived at home, we used to watch lots of slasher movies, and his VCR always had problems. Anyway, I got up to check it out, but she grabbed my wrist and pulled me back onto the couch.

"My life is a total disaster!"

"What? Why?"

"I'm getting held back a year. I'll have to spend a whole year with kids a year younger than me. It's gonna be horrible!"

"But I thought you weren't worried about that. You ..."

"And my boyfriend is just as dumb as I am," she interrupted.

She had tears in her eyes. "Just as dumb," she repeated. She said that things had been different since Schulz had hit her. She couldn't get over it, and she didn't want to. Besides, she said, they weren't really a good match for each other. All he ever talked about was money, cars, and everything he was going to buy her. I tried to be understanding. I told her that the money wasn't really that important, in the end, and that what really mattered was us—all of us. At that moment I meant it, too. Her hand moved, slowly, from her knee to mine. Her fingers looked so delicate. I took her thumb and gently pushed it backward. At first it was just, I don't know, a thoughtless reaction, but her thumb just kept going back as I added more pressure, so that in the end it was almost at a right angle. It was crazy.

"What the hell, Lena? What's with your thumb?"

"Yeah, it's funny, right? Look, the other one does it, too. But only if I do it."

The sadness melted away from her voice. She pulled one leg up onto the couch, turned her body toward me, and holding her other thumb in front of my nose, she bent it back ninety degrees. When she pulled her hand away again, her face was only inches away from mine. She came closer; it just happened. Her lips were soft, and I just barely brushed the tip of her tongue with mine. It was a cautious kiss because I remembered reading somewhere that it was better to be too careful than too pushy. It wasn't like we were at some wild party; this was her house. Lena stood up, put some soft rock on the stereo, and sat down again next to me.

We moved to the bed. Lena kept the CD on, and the lame music ruined the mood a little. I guess it was kind of romantic, but we weren't in love, and we definitely weren't a couple. But here I was in this important moment, listening to Bryan Adams singing "Everything I Do."

PHILIPP MATTHEIS

I'd been carrying a condom in my wallet for the last six months, and now, finally, I got to actually use it. I moved on top of her, trying to keep a pretty steady rhythm. She said "faster" and I went faster, but then she asked me to slow down again and that was much more difficult. A few minutes, and it was all over.

It's hard to describe what I was feeling, and it's hard to explain why it felt so monumental, but it changed everything. I'd actually done it. I wasn't a virgin anymore. That was important. But it was also important because I was starting to realize that I didn't just think Lena was "cool." I actually liked her.

We lay on top of the comforter and smoked. The afternoon sun warmed our skin, and outside we could hear the kids in a nearby playground. I wanted to ask her if it was any different than with Schulz. But I stopped myself; I got the impression that it hadn't been as important for her as it was for me. So I didn't say anything. Lena's head was resting on my shoulder, and her blonde hair was spread over my chest. I couldn't help myself and kissed her just under her ear. She said that it tickled.

After we'd finished smoking, Lena stood up and threw the window wide open. Then she sprayed a perfume through the room and waved it around with her hand. It smelled like strawberries.

"My mom will flip out if she realizes we smoked in here. She'll take away my allowance."

What did that matter though? I still had a thick bundle of cash lying in my desk drawer. It wasn't as thick as before, maybe, but there was still enough to cover any expenses. Come to think of it, I'd actually been spending a lot lately. In the last few weeks I'd bought about a thousand marks' worth of clothes—that was the only big expense I could allow myself without my parents getting suspicious. The rest had gone for . . . well, for what? Taxis, pizzas, cigarettes, alcohol, tips—stuff like that. Several thousand marks in a few weeks. I don't think she would have really wanted any of my money anyway.

I stood up and got dressed. Every so often there would be a *pft pft*, and the room would light up with the smell of strawberries. I wrinkled my nose.

"This is the one Schulzie got me. He thought he had to get me something. But I hate Opium. I wanted the one from Calvin Klein. It smells awful, right?"

I nodded. I didn't really want to think about Schulz just then.

"By the way, just so that we're clear: What happened today stays between us. I don't want people thinking I'm the school slut or anything."

A gust of wind blew through the room. With a quick motion, she slipped her hair three times through a black rubber band. All of a sudden she was in control again.

"Okay," I said.

"Promise?"

I nodded.

She left to go to the bathroom. I waited for her on the bed.

"I've gotta go now," she said when she returned. She'd gotten dressed and put makeup on. Now she was wearing a black miniskirt instead of the jeans. "I'm meeting up with Sarah."

She kissed me on the cheek and somehow made me understand that I was the one who was supposed to go. I pressed her hand and left the house.

On my way home, the first waves of guilt started to crash over me. The more I thought about it, the more helpless I felt. No matter how you looked at it, I was definitely in the wrong. Despite all their fighting, Lena and Schulz were still officially a couple, and to make matters worse, he was still my friend. I'm not sure what happened next, but something inside me definitely changed. I guess it was maybe a function of the fact that so much seemed out of control: Sam was losing it, Eric had his own crazy plans, and sooner or later, me and Lena wouldn't be able to stay friends because she was my friend's girlfriend and I'd just slept with her. Considering everything that was happening, it would have been surprising if I *didn't* kind of lose my shit.

When I got home, it was late afternoon and my parents weren't home yet. I took Hilda Stetlow's letters out and struggled to make sense of her spidery handwriting again. I was hoping that I might find something new. Then I took the rubber band off the bundle of bills and counted them. Their coating of dust was disgusting, which meant that I couldn't lick my fingers to gain a better grip. So I fumbled through the bills, counted, miscounted, and started over again. When I was finished I had a total of forty-six hundred marks. I lay on my bed and stared at the ceiling.

The money had to go. It had to go. Far, far away. The letters, too. The sooner, the better. I wanted everything to go back to the way it was before.

I went to the kitchen and got some plastic bags. Then I got a garden trowel from the garage and headed out. I hadn't used my bike in ages. At first the motion felt strange because it was literally the first time I'd ridden it since I was about twelve. I knew where I was going now. I was heading to the duck blind.

Fifteen minutes later, I was standing in the woods about a mile out of town. The sun filtered through the leaves and the pine needles in thin beams. I could hear a bird cooing somewhere close by in a strangely deep tone. It smelled like moss and trees. The ground sank down a little with every step I took; cracking twigs broke the silence. I looked around and made sure that there was no one watching me. It was the right thing to do, the money had to be buried. Lena was right; it brought bad luck. It had to disappear. This was the only way everything could return to normal again.

As much as I hoped that would be true, I also knew that you can't turn back time. I made my way over to the duck blind and—like pirates in movies always do—I took seven big steps to the right. I stopped in front of an over-sized tree root and looked around, making sure I could remember the exact spot. Then I used my hand to sweep aside all the little leaves and pine needles until I could feel the dirt. The soil was dark and damp. No one would look here, no one.

I started to dig. Not too deep, but deep enough that you would never be able to see the plastic. About eight inches. An earthworm turned away against the flood of light.

Now, even if anyone found the money, it couldn't be linked to me. The police couldn't launch an investigation with just a wad of cash. I saw more worms, beetles, and other insects that I couldn't name. There, in that unsecured damp hive of activity, I left the plastic bag with the letters and four thousand marks. No one would ever find it now, not even by accident. When I'd refilled the hole with dirt and covered it with pine needles and leaves, I stood up, took a few steps backward, and made sure I'd memorized the spot. Seven steps to the right from the right-hand front corner of the duck blind. Right in front of a fat tree root.

It was done. I'd buried my money in the ground.

I wanted to give away everything I still owned.

Then I would be free.

＊ ＊ ＊

When I got back home, I called Daniel. It had been a while since we had talked. He picked up after the eighth ring. I told him what had happened with Lena. Twenty minutes later I was standing at his front door.

"Well done," he said.

He held out his hand and I shook it. He turned around jerkily and scurried back to the couch and his Play-Station. I sat down next to him.

"How was it?"

I shrugged because I really wasn't sure whether it had been good or not. I guess you can only say that about something when you have something to compare it to, and this was just my first time.

He grinned.

"Hey man," I said, making an effort to look serious, "how are you doing cash-wise? Wanna borrow some money? I'm loaded right now."

I didn't wait for his answer, just handed him five bills. All I had left now was a single hundred-mark bill in my wallet. It might seem dumb to go to all those lengths and then still hold on to some of the cash, but it was a hundred marks, and that was still a lot of money. The five bills disappeared into Daniel's wallet. With that done, we sat and played *Streetfighter 2*. Daniel won.

SEVENTEEN

"C-c-can you bring some money with you?"

Sam's voice rattled like a faulty car engine.

"I still need c-c-cash for beer and other s-stuff."

"I've hardly got any left," I answered. "And what 'other stuff'?"

"Eric has, E-Eric has, E-, I shouldn't talk about it like this." He was whispering through the receiver.

"Are you serious? Why are you whispering? Sam?"

More low noises.

"Sam? I didn't catch that."

The sound was replaced by the dial tone. He'd hung up. Why had he been whispering? It had been Eric and Schulz's idea to have a little party at Sam's place. They'd suggested that he have a "session," and Sam had gone along with the idea. Once we'd made the plan, though, all three of us had each told other people about it, so now Sam didn't have any idea how many people were actually planning on coming over later that night. (His parents were on vacation in Italy, on Lake Garda, where they went every summer. Sam had been home alone for a week.)

Sam's parents' house was pretty far away, on a street at the edge of town that only had houses on one side. On the other side was a cornfield, where the corn was now taller than we were. It was late afternoon and the sun was shining diagonally through the plants' deep green leaves. It seemed like vacation had just started. In a few weeks the field would be harvested, and then summer would be over.

Behind the field, back toward the woods, there was an old barn. That was where Sam and I had gone to smoke our very first cigarettes together. He'd made fun of me because I had just puffed on them instead of inhaling into my lungs. After chain-smoking three, I'd felt sick and thrown up on the wall of the barn. We laughed about it now.

I opened the short cast-iron gate and walked up the driveway and over to the patio. Eric was sitting in a rickety, brightly patterned lawn chair. His feet were on a footstool, and he was almost lying down. Only his right arm was up, supported by the back of the chair, to hold a cigarette. Schulz was sitting next to him with his Ray-Bans on. My pulse sped up when I saw him. I was glad I couldn't see his eyes. I'd been avoiding him ever since my thing with Lena, but he didn't know anything, he couldn't know anything. It was our secret.

With a smile on his face, Eric held out his hand for me to shake. On the table was a bag of weed, slightly smaller than the one from the park in Munich, and next to it was a palm-sized clump of hash and a small bag with a pile of little red tablets inside. They were about the size of aspirin and had a symbol on them that I didn't recognize. There was also a packet with little blue capsules that looked like hard candy.

"What's that?" I asked, pointing to the bag with the red pills.

Schulz giggled.

"That's E," said Eric with a grin.

"And those?"

Schulz emitted a sudden burst of laughter, with little drops of spit darting out of his mouth. Then it turned into a tinny laugh. *Hekhekhekhekhekhek.* Eric joined in, too, less annoyingly. He stretched out further in the lawn chair.

"They're microdots."

"Microdots?"

Eric nodded.

"Okay . . . What are microdots?"

Schulz was laughing so hard he grabbed his stomach. His skinny body was shaking and contorting.

"Microdots," said Eric, laughing. "Microdots are like tickets, but stronger."

"Tickets?"

"LSD, retard."

"Whatever. Where's Sam?"

Schulz could hardly breathe.

"Sam's in kind of a weird mood," said Eric. "First of all, he took three—" *Hekhekhekhekhekhek*. He was interrupted by another roar of laughter from Schulz. "First of all, he took three microdots."

"Three," Schulz cackled. "He had three! Three!"

"He took three microdots and then he went upstairs and pulled down all the blinds. We don't know why. The whole time he was muttering about something, but we couldn't understand him." *Okay*, I thought, *that explains things*.

I went through the patio door and into the house. Schulz's laughter grew quieter. In the living room, CDs and clothes were scattered all around the floor. I picked up a Doors CD and put it on. Outside, Schulz was still cackling. "When summer's gone, where will we be?" Jim Morrison sang—*hekhekhekhek*. It felt like we were in a movie and this was the soundtrack: Eric, Sam, Schulz, me—we were all like actors who did what we did because it was in the script. And now, here in Sam's house, with the Doors playing—somehow it all fit together. Except it was sort of sad and fucked up. You always want everything to be like in a movie, but when it happens, then you just want to go back to normal again. At least that's what I wanted because here, now, it was all too much for me.

The kitchen was a mess. Beer and wine bottles were everywhere, along with pizza boxes and ice-cream cartons. It stank. Over by the staircase it was already dark. I had to turn the lights on. Clothes were strewn over the stairs: T-shirts, boxer shorts, Sam's Yankees cap. When I got to the top, I went to Sam's room. The blinds were all down, and the room would have been pitch black except for a candle stub burning in the middle. It was light enough for me to see that Sam wasn't there. In the next room, his parents' bedroom, it was the same: The room was dark except for a small candle. Even the bathroom had a candle in it.

Someone had scrawled something on the mirror with a marker, but I couldn't make it out. The words didn't make any sense. Back in the hallway, I could hear him. He came toward me, but he didn't see me. His head was lowered, and he was carrying a candle and a lighter, whose wheel he kept spinning, making little sparks spray out. He hissed, muttered, and whispered. He smelled like he hadn't showered in days.

I called his name. He didn't react; it was like he hadn't heard me.

"Sam!" I said again. He muttered, but still didn't respond. He acted like he was talking to someone who wasn't there. I grabbed his arm. Gently, but firmly. His upper body jerked as if I'd interrupted him during an important task. His head snapped up, but he seemed to look straight through me.

"*Sam*!" I said.

Slowly, very slowly, his eyes began to focus on me. It seemed to dawn on him gradually.

"What are you doing? What's with the candles and the blinds?"

He hissed something at me. It sounded like "vshshsst."

"What?"

He did it again. "Vshshsst."

Then he muttered, almost coherently, "Leave me alone." He turned his back to me, and I could see dust and bits of wax on his jacket. I wanted to stop him, but I realized that I probably couldn't make any difference. It was like he wasn't even there. He kept arranging candles and talking to the creatures in his own horrible world. I went down the steps, through the living room, and back onto the patio, into the open, the fresh air, the sun. Schulz and Eric were still in the same spot, smoking cigarettes. I sat down between them, took a beer from the box, and started rolling a joint.

"Why did you let him take so much?" I asked.

"What do you want me to do?" Eric said. "I was just being nice!"

Schulz burst into laughter again.

"He saw them and stuffed three of them in his mouth. I told him, 'Sam, just take one.' But he wanted three. There was nothing we could do to stop him. He was totally nuts about it."

"I think he's lost it. He doesn't respond when you talk to him."

"Just let him spin out a little. He'll come down soon."

"What if he doesn't?"

"Then he should drink milk. Or take vitamin C. That'll make you come down. That's what Zafko does, and he knows what he's doing with that shit."

I turned and looked at Schulz. He was still giggling to himself. He wasn't good enough for Lena. Anyone who could sit there with a pair of three-hundred-mark sunglasses and giggle to himself for half an hour was a total retard.

So we sat there for an hour or two: Schulz giggled, Eric smiled, I stewed in my anger and frustration, and the sun slowly sank into the cornfield.

* * *

The cast-iron gate creaked and Lena came through. She was wearing a short black summer dress, the same one she'd been wearing when I'd seen her at the train station. Her friend Sarah was with her. They came to the patio and noticed Eric's smorgasbord of drugs.

"What the hell is all this?" Lena asked, pointing to the table. She didn't look at me or Schulz. He'd stopped giggling by now.

"Oh, that was just sitting there when we got here," said Eric, without the slightest change in his king-on-a-throne attitude.

"Right."

Sarah took a bottle of Kahlua out of her handbag, and the two of them went to get glasses from the filthy kitchen. I watched them when they came back. Maybe if I hadn't smoked any pot, I could have gone over to them, said something witty, made them laugh, and then sat with them. But that was pretty much out of the question. It was sure to go wrong. My tongue felt like a piece of chalk, and even if I thought of something interesting to say—or, better yet, something funny—they wouldn't understand it, and they'd have to ask me to repeat it, and I would have to give the punch line again, and then it would be completely ridiculous and embarrassing . . . Anyway, Schulz would see us. When I looked at him, my thoughts got all tangled up.

By about midnight the yard was filled with twenty or so people. Even Carina was there. I guess Daniel had invited her. She gave me a little nod when she saw me, and I nodded back. I thought it would be better not to talk to her. Jim, the punk kid, was lighting a fire on the compost heap. He'd found a gasoline container in the garage and was sprinkling the contents over the rotted food and yard waste. It wouldn't be long before he'd start in on his standard battle cry: "Anarchy! Anarchy!"

Small groups of kids sat on the gradually dampening grass and drank. Daniel lounged for hours in a chair next to Schulz and Eric, smoking. Someone brought the stereo speakers onto the patio, and now a Snoop Dogg album was reverberating through the yard and the cornfield. Which, when you thought about it, was kind of strange, considering that Snoop Dogg lived in South Central LA, and here we were in front of a cornfield in a suburb of Munich. Eric and Schulz hadn't said anything for the last hour. They just stared into the clear night sky with their mouths hanging open or laughed about something that only they understood. I watched Schulz's face. He didn't look at me. He didn't know. He couldn't know. It probably wouldn't matter to him anyway. If Lena meant anything to him, he wouldn't be sitting on a stupid lawn chair, tripping. That's what I told myself. If he really loved her, he would talk to her, take care of her, make her laugh. They hadn't said a single word to each other the whole night. Their relationship was broken, and I had just sped up the process.

Lena and Sarah were talking with two guys I'd never seen before. I looked around and realized that I actually only knew half the people there.

"Who are all these people?" I asked Daniel. "Like those guys over there." I pointed to the two guys talking to Lena. "I've never seen them before."

Daniel shrugged.

"No idea. Maybe Lena brought them, or maybe Sam invited them. Where is Sam, anyway?"

I didn't know. I hadn't seen him for hours. He hadn't come outside, even though this was supposed to be his party. We'd forgotten all about him. No one cared, as long as there was enough music, alcohol, and whatever else. A couple of times I heard people asking why the whole second floor was dark.

There was a loud, hollow bang. Girls screamed, Schulz jumped, and Eric sprang out of his chair. All of a sudden the yard was lit up. Flames shot three feet into the air. Someone shouted, "You maniacs!"

"Anarchy!" Jim yelled.

"Fucking punk!" someone shouted. The compost heap was a huge fireball. Schulz whimpered, scrunched up in a ball in an LSD-fueled haze. People freaked out at first, but as the initial anxiety subsided, everyone thought it was pretty awesome, too.

Eric stood in front of his chair, gaping. It took a few seconds for him to realize what was happening. Then he sat back down to enjoy the show. Two girls danced around the fire. A couple of drunk guys started chanting, and Jim positioned himself as close as possible to the flames and sprinkled more gas onto it.

I don't really know why I stood up just then. It wasn't like me to do something like that—to join in, I mean. I stumbled over to Lena and Sarah and the two guys. In the corner of the yard the blaze flared. I could feel the heat. They fell silent when I got there. The two guys were a full head taller than me, and they must have been at least five years older. They wore collared shirts under their sweaters. Their jeans fit perfectly, not an inch too big, and on their feet were shiny black leather shoes. Awkwardly, I reached for Lena's hand. I didn't care if Schulz saw. Let them all see, Schulz, Eric, Carina, and especially this douchebag standing next to her. She pulled her hand away.

"We were just about to leave."

"Who's we?"

The two guys looked me up and down.

"Alex and Dave are taking us to Nightflight."

"'Alex and Dave'? Are you serious?"

One of them said, "Lena, this guy's wasted. Let's go."

"I'm not wasted . . . you fucking douchebag," I said.

He took a step toward me. I took a step back. He suddenly looked even taller. His friend grabbed his shoulder and said something quietly that I didn't hear.

"Leave him alone, Dave. He's drunk," said Lena.

"I'm not drunk! Who is this guy, anyway?"

"We're leaving. Don't make a scene," she said.

"You're leaving with these homos? Who are they? Where do you know them from?"

"Lena," said the other one, "I'm not about to take crap from some drunk kid. I've got better things to do."

Lena grabbed me by the arm and pulled me away.

"I told you before: What happened the other day was a one-time thing, okay? You're a nice guy, but nothing's ever going to happen between us. Got it? I'm sorry I have to say it like that. But you don't seem to get it. Dave's a nice guy and he's gonna get us into Nightflight, so just leave it alone. Okay?"

"Fucking assholes!"

The four of them got into a black Jeep Wrangler. At first I was just going to leave it, but then something came over me, and I ran down the driveway and after the Jeep as they pulled away. After a few yards, I stopped and flung my beer bottle at the car, even though only the taillights were still visible. It shattered on the asphalt.

I went back. Just as I pulled the cast-iron gate shut behind me, another car pulled up and parked in front of the house. A police car. Two middle-aged officers, both in black leather jackets, got out. One of them had a thick moustache. They came straight toward me.

"Can I see some ID?"

I pulled my ID out of my wallet, which still had the old hundred-mark bill in it. While one cop took my ID back to the car, the other asked me if this was my party. I said no.

"We've had a complaint about the noise. And," he paused, his gaze coming to rest on the bonfire. "And it looks like we might also have a case of arson. Oliver!" he called to his partner. "Call the fire department. We've gotta get that put out."

He turned back to me. "Whose party is this?"

"My friend's. Sam's," I answered meekly.

"Does Sam have a full name?"

"Samuel Meyer."

"And where is Samuel Meyer?"

I pointed to the house. "Um, inside somewhere."

His partner gave me my ID back.

"No history," he said.

"Okay. Let's go talk to Mr. Meyer."

As I walked back into the yard with the cops, chaos broke out. Joints were extinguished, beers were poured out over the fire (which did absolutely nothing to diminish it), couples stopped making out, liquor bottles landed in the shrubs—the party was over. On the patio, Eric was tucking bags into his pockets. The police headed straight toward him.

"Are you Samuel Meyer?" the one with the moustache asked Eric.

"Nope," answered Eric. "Are you?"

Daniel giggled.

The cop looked at Eric. "Get your ID out."

The one with the moustache positioned himself on the patio, turned to the drugged-up crowd, and said loudly, "We're looking for Samuel Meyer. Can he please step forward."

Some people started whispering but no one answered.

"Samuel Meyer!" the cop called again. Then he got angrier: "If no one steps forward, then we'll take down information for everyone here. Including all those who are underage. Which one of you is Samuel Meyer?"

Silence.

Eric was still fishing for his ID, doing his best to keep the contents of his pockets from spilling out.

"He's upstairs," said Daniel.

"What?"

"I think he's upstairs," Daniel repeated.

"Why don't you come with us, too." He looked suspiciously at Daniel, clearly noticing how small he was. "And let's see some ID." Daniel pulled out his license. After looking it over, the cops headed upstairs. Daniel followed. So did I.

* * *

The entire floor was dark except for flickering candles. "What's going on up here?" the mustached one asked. We didn't answer.

They went from door to door, opening them and shining their flashlights in. It was clear they weren't too impressed.

They found Sam in the bathroom. He was crouched down in the bathtub with a knife in his hand, waving it around like he was fighting demons or something. Except for the knife, he looked completely harmless; completely helpless.

"Are you Samuel Meyer?"

Sam didn't answer. Then again, no one ever called him "Samuel." The knife moved aimlessly through the air.

"We've had a complaint about the noise."

Sam's clouded eyes seemed to register the cops.

"You, you, you," he said, and then he hissed, "Ge-get out! Y-y-you sent them! G-go away! Go away! Get out!"

Sam stood up and pointed the knife toward the policemen. I could tell he wanted to say something, but he only produced hissing noises. Little bubbles of spit formed in the corners of his mouth, and more trickled down his chin and got caught in his stubble. He raised the knife up over his head, and the mustached cop lifted his gun out of its holster. Sam was about six feet from the officers and lifting his leg to step out of the tub.

"Don't!" shrieked Daniel at the policemen. "He's sick!"

"Mr. Meyer, stop. Can you hear us?" the other cop said.

Sam paused, hissing and whispering, eyes scanning the air in confusion. He focused briefly and then was lost again.

"Sam!" I shouted. "Put the knife down!" I took a step toward him, but the policeman held me back.

"Don't shoot," said Daniel again. He was pleading like a little kid. "Don't shoot."

In one smooth movement, the policeman wrapped his arm around Sam's wrist and closed on it, tight. Sam cried out sharply, like a rat, but before he could try to free himself, the policeman's other hand covered the hand holding the kitchen knife. With some sort of special police grip, he turned Sam's wrist so that he dropped the knife.

Seconds later, Sam's wrists were bound by handcuffs. As Sam alternated whimpers with screams, the mustached cop radioed for an ambulance.

EIGHTEEN

I didn't find out until days later, but the next day Sam was admitted to a psychiatric hospital. I had called his house to check on him, to ask where he'd been; so much had happened, and I needed to talk. His dad answered the phone. "Paranoid schizophrenia," he said, and something about "persecutory delusions." His voice wasn't friendly. I hung up figuring I should leave Sam alone for a little while until he was back again.

The night of the party, after the firefighters had put out the compost fire, the police had sent everyone home. No one was arrested, and no one was responsible enough to clean up the mess. We figured the police would bring Sam back in a few hours, or the next day, once he'd come down from his trip. Eric told us he was going to see Zafko;

he had to talk to him about some business. After he left, Schulz came up to me. He seemed confused, as if he'd just woken up from a long dream.

"Where's Lena? Why isn't she here?"

I shook my head and went home.

* ̣ ◆

I slept badly that night. When I did doze off for an hour or two, my dreaming was cloudy and confused. It didn't fit together—it was like scraps of images that collided together and then fell apart. I only remembered some of it later. I was sitting at the wheel of a car, with Lena next to me, careening through our suburb of Meining at ninety miles an hour. There were no brakes, and I couldn't tell what all the buttons and knobs were for. I tried to concentrate and keep the car in control, but it was hopeless. Meanwhile, Lena was just sitting there, calm but clearly annoyed, almost grimacing even. We sped toward the church with its big steeple. But then everything changed. Eric was standing in front of me, reaching into a bag of colorful pills and shoving a handful of them into his mouth. His teeth were fanged, like an animal's.

Then Sam came running toward me. He said that we had to leave—that two sisters were after him. "Every second counts," he said. I tried to calm him down, telling him we should stop and think about what to do next. He shouted, "No, we have to go *now*!"

Then I smelled them. They smelled like mildew, just like the house. Panicking, we ran as fast as we could, but at some point Sam stopped running. He was rooted to the ground, panting, gasping for air. I called to him, "Run!" But he couldn't manage it. They kept coming, though. They were going to get him.

The next thing I knew I was sitting on the couch at Daniel's house. "Everyone knows that the house is cursed," he said. "Everyone knows. You guys were the only ones who didn't. Because you didn't want to know . . . It's your own fault, isn't it?"

I'm not sure why I went back to the house. Maybe I wanted some sort of closure. Maybe it wasn't enough to just bury the money. I don't know. The only thing I am sure of is that I wasn't looking for more cash. Even if I found some, I wasn't going to take it. I was after something else.

Maybe I just wanted to see the house with fresh eyes.

I rode my bike to Flower Street. The summer had passed since we'd last been there. The hedge was yellow in some places and brown in others. It smelled like fall. It was totally silent; I was alone. The gap in the hedge was much bigger now. You could see it easily if you were just walking past.

I rounded the house and stood at the back by the open patio door. A few shards of glass lay on the moss-covered stones. In the middle of the glass door was a gaping hole. Someone had thrown a rock through the pane of glass. The clothesline wasn't hanging up anymore either.

It was on the ground, along with the apron and the bag of colorful clothespins.

I went up the stairs to the living area. The key was still in the door, just like last time. I took it out. Inside was the same smell of mildew. I used the key to lock the door from the inside. There was a general air of menace, and I have to admit, I was kind of afraid.

No one else was here, I reminded myself. I was alone. No one would bother me.

The entire floor was a complete mess. It was total chaos. Just papers, towels, filth, and broken furniture. A bookshelf had been turned over and was leaning against the opposite wall, and the tattered books were lying on the floor. The whole second story was covered in a layer of personal papers, yellowed newspapers, clothing, and bed linens—in places, you were standing a good six inches off the actual floor. I stepped over a shattered teapot from the kitchen. Since we'd been there, every room had been completely ransacked.

I went into the bedroom where we'd found the sixty thousand marks. I moved slowly and cautiously, like a detective at a crime scene, careful not to disturb any evidence. There were feathers everywhere: brown, white, and gray down feathers. The wardrobe was destroyed, its door split to pieces, and the contents—all the bed linens and blouses—had been thrown to the ground and ripped up into tatters.

The living room was in even worse shape: The glass doors on the china cabinet had been shattered—probably with the ax, which was lying on the floor, surrounded by shards of glass, porcelain, and crystal. A broken violin had been tossed in the corner. The sofa and the armchairs were turned over, all of them slashed open. Whoever it was, whether they found anything or not, they must have decided to just trash the place for good measure. The entire second floor was a dump.

Was it Strasser? Had there been any money left to find? I was thinking about how angry and frustrated these guys must have been when I heard a sudden, sharp, cracking sound, like the popping of somebody's arthritic knee. I froze. Then I heard a scratching sound, then more cracking, and then scratching again. It was hard to tell where the noise was coming from. I didn't move, I barely breathed, turning my full attention to the noise. It was quiet for a moment, but then it started up again: the scratching of gravel on concrete and the cracking of old bones.

Someone was coming up the stairs.

Someone else was in the house.

A woman's voice—an old woman's voice—said "Hello?" She sounded like an out-of-tune violin.

"Is anybody there?" the old woman asked.

She sounded sick and helpless. Where had she come from? Then it hit me: the basement. Sam must have seen her that day when he went down into the basement. That's what he'd been running from. I wasn't sure what to do. I stared at the broken violin on the floor. I was sweating. I could hear the doorknob: An old, rusty spring tightened slowly, steel rubbing on steel, very deliberately, almost tenderly. A lurch. And then another. It didn't open.

"Hello?" she croaked again.

She paused, clearly listening on the other side. The seconds stretched out, with only my breathing to mark the time.

I don't know how long we stood like that. But after a long, long silence, I heard the scratch and crackle again. She was heading back downstairs.

Outside, a dog started barking. I hardly moved until I couldn't hear the sounds from Hilda's retreat anymore. I listened carefully: no more noise, no cracking or scratching or dogs barking. Still, I was too afraid to move. Then I thought, what if she gets nervous and calls the police? Then I'd be really trapped. I had to get out of that house.

As quietly as I could, I tiptoed to the door. Like a mountain climber, I planned out every step. I silently made my way past papers, clothes, and dishes. I pressed my ear against the door, listened, and then turned the key in slow motion. The metal cracked a little as the bolt snapped. Carefully I turned the knob. The spring inside tightened, and finally the door opened.

I peeked through the opening and looked down the staircase. No one, nothing. I opened the door wider, just enough to slip my body through. I tiptoed down the staircase to the first floor. I wanted to run, but I moved cautiously and quietly to the patio door, slid it open, and stepped outside.

At that point, I bent over and hurried through the yard, burst through the hedge, and leapt on my bike, riding as fast as I could away from Flower Street. I didn't turn around once, not even to make sure that no one had seen me. I just stared at the pavement and pedalled as fast as I could.

Never again, I swore to myself. That was the last time I would ever go on that street. The last time I'd ever so much as look at that house. It was over. It was over forever. The sky grew dark as I rode home. Finally, I lay down in bed and rolled a joint with the little bit of weed I had left. Then it started to rain.

* * *

About midnight, the phone rang. Fat drops were falling from the sky. I'd had the TV on for hours, trying to distract myself. It was Lena. Within seconds I knew she wasn't calling to talk about us, or about the guys from Sam's party, or about Terminal.

There was no fake voice. No "Yeah, hiii, it's Lenaaa." Just a quick "Hi," then a pause, then: "There was an accident. It's Schulz."

She said that Schulz's parents had called her parents with the news. Schulz had been on his way over to her house—in a stolen car. He'd finally done it, after talking about it for so long. One time he'd seen a friend from another school do it. He'd opened the door with a piece of wire hanger, and from there it was a no-brainer.

Anyway, Schulz had gotten it in Munich, the neighborhood near Terminal, Lena said. The police weren't sure exactly what happened; they didn't have any witnesses to the accident. But Schulz's blood had tested positive for alcohol, and the police had also found cocaine in the car.

She was clearly leaving something out. I started to ask, "Is he . . . ," and she immediately broke down in tears. Full sobs. She cried, gasped for air, cried again. She only stopped to blow her nose. After a few minutes, she composed herself enough to say, "He was coming to see me. He'd told his mom he was going to spend the night here. But he didn't say anything to me. We hadn't talked in days. The last time we saw each other was Sam's."

She didn't say the words, but I understood. I swallowed a few times, but the lump in my throat didn't go away. He was dead. Schulz was dead. The finality of that sunk into my soul like dropping a rock into a bottomless well; it just fell and fell. I'd never known anyone who'd died. Not even my grandparents. I couldn't feel any change. Everything was exactly the same: I was lying in my bed talking to Lena. The TV was on mute. Rain clattered against the window. Nothing was different except that Schulz was now gone forever. "He was the only one I really loved."

Lena repeated this four or five times. Each time her voice got quieter, until she fell totally silent. We sat in silence, listening to each other breathing, for probably five minutes. Then she inhaled and exhaled deeply and said, "I've got to get some sleep."

I said good night, and we hung up.

I wasn't sure what I was supposed to do. I didn't know how I was supposed to feel. Death is strange. Schulz was gone, but if I hadn't been told he was dead, I might have imagined that he had just run off—to Brazil or Japan or somewhere. I would have preferred that.

I searched deep inside myself, trying to find what I was supposed to feel, waiting for the tears to come.

NINETEEN

Daniel's mom was a short, round woman with a short hair-cut that hugged her friendly, happy face. She wore a pair of glasses with lenses as round as she was, and I couldn't help thinking that she looked a little like a hobbit. She smiled at me mischievously as she opened the door.

"You're Jonathan, aren't you?"

"Yes," I answered shyly, tacking on a "How are you?"

"Jonathan," she said, "the next time you have a party, please don't leave your trash in the houseplants. I'd ap-preciate it."

I wanted to say that I didn't have any idea what she was talking about, it wasn't me, I had nothing to do with any of that. But she smiled and said, "Daniel is upstairs in his room." I nodded.

I glanced around the living room. The leather couch was clean; the blanket that Daniel always wrapped around himself was folded neatly in the corner. The glass table sparkled and held a few magazines. The TV was gray and silent. It was hard to believe this was the same room where we smoked, played video games, and partied not long ago. I climbed up the hardwood stairs and opened the door to Daniel's room. He was sitting on his bed, his hat pulled down over his leprechaun face, a controller in his hand.

"Are you in trouble with your parents? Your mom just asked me not to leave any trash in the houseplants."

"Really? I bet the cleaning lady must've said something."

He concentrated on his game. I watched him play until he lost. He swore, tossed the controller on the bed, and looked at me.

"Daniel," I said, "did you hear about . . ."

"Eric? Yeah. But hey, that was gonna happen sooner or later. Everyone knew that he was dealing. I mean, if you're gonna go around town with a bag of weed and ask thirteen-year-olds if they want to buy any, then you can't be surprised when shit hits the fan, right?"

My eyes widened as something in me sank down. My stomach started to churn.

"So they . . . ?"

"They caught him. You didn't know about it?"

I shook my head.

"Some seventh-grader probably told his parents that a tall guy with a backpack was asking him if he wanted to buy weed. The cops found him yesterday at the station, waiting for the train. And get this: He tried to run away. Like he's in some kind of movie! Eric runs down the track toward the city, and the cops start chasing him with their guns drawn. They're shouting, 'Stop! Stop or we'll shoot!' So he gets rid of his backpack and just keeps going. At some point, I guess he wussed out or he couldn't run anymore. They put him in handcuffs and took him away. Do you know how much they found on him? Half a pound! He had half a pound in his backpack, plus pills and who knows what else. As far as I know, he's still in custody. They're keeping him till someone posts his bail or something. He's sitting in jail right this second. Can you believe it?"

The money, I thought. The house, the money, the woods, the old lady's voice.

"How did you . . . ?"

"Jim told me. He's always hanging out around the train station. He was there. He saw everything happen. Eric just took it too far. That's Eric. He's always overdoing it. He should have been more careful. Never—I've always said this—never sell to kids. That's the riskiest thing you can do. If anyone's gonna talk, it'll be one of them. They act like they're cool, but really they're just scared shitless. As soon as their mom suspects anything, they start talking."

"What if Eric talks?"

"If he even mentions Zafko, he's gonna be in deep shit. I don't even want to know what kind of people Zafko knows. If Eric tells the cops that he bought from Zafko, he's an idiot. He'll have a huge fucking problem when he gets out. I wouldn't put anything past Zafko. Eric might get off on probation, if he's lucky. But Zafko is an adult, he's twenty-three or maybe even older. They'd book him. If I were Eric, I'd start thinking up a good story. Plus, yeah, there's all that with the house, too. But he's not stupid enough to tell them about that."

He picked up the controller to start another round. I punched him on the shoulder.

"How do you know about the house?! I can't believe you know about it. You knew the whole time, didn't you?"

"Of course, I knew about it. Everyone knew about it."

"Everyone?"

"Okay, maybe not everyone. But ever since the thing with Strasser, it was like an open secret. Do you seriously think that no one's gonna notice when you're throwing around these huge wads of cash? Carina knew, Strasser knew, even Jim knew—and normally he doesn't know much of anything because he's always drunk. You guys weren't exactly making an effort to keep it a secret. You yourself gave me five hundred marks. You think I'm stupid? Anyway, everyone in Meining already knew about the house. Even my mom. Your face looks really pale, by the way. Go look in a mirror."

He pressed start and began to fight. His fingers mashed the buttons chaotically. His body moved right and left, as if he could use his own weight to move the character. I stood up, opened the door to the balcony, and lit a cigarette. The money was buried. They wouldn't find anything at my house. If Eric tried to rat me out, I could always deny it. They couldn't prove anything. No one had seen me; there were no witnesses. Well, Schulz couldn't talk, but Sam . . . He was in a psych ward. Would anyone believe him? What good would it do Eric to throw me under the bus?

"Did you say that your mom knew about the house?"

Daniel kept playing, as if he hadn't heard my question. After a few more minutes of combat, he put the controller aside and turned to face me.

"I don't actually know all the details. It was a few years ago. I was still in grade school. I heard my mom talking with our neighbor, Mrs. Dullinger, and she said that one of the sisters in the house on Flower Street had died and that the other sister was crazy. That wasn't a surprise. Everyone in our neighborhood knew that she was bonkers. Maybe it was a head injury from World War II or something, who knows. But she was definitely pretty crazy. She thought people were out to get her."

"Out to get her? Do you know who she thought was following her?"

Daniel kept talking as if he hadn't heard me. "I was about seven or eight when I first noticed her. She acted weirdly around dogs. She was scared of them. She would cross to the other side of the street when she saw someone walking their dog. Sometimes she would start swearing at the dogs, just going off on them. Obviously people in this neighborhood didn't really like that, since pretty much everyone has a dog. She would curse them out, scream at them, wave her cane at them. People started talking about her and telling their kids to stay away from her. My mom told me that Mrs. Stetlow was sick and that she really needed help. But my mom was probably the only one who felt sympathetic toward her. Most of our neighbors just bitched about her. And honestly, I thought she was creepy. I was scared of her. She was ugly, and her wrinkled little face sort of fell down around her mouth because she didn't have any teeth. Her hair was a mess. She was always wearing dirty aprons. And she always stank of sweat and rotten food."

I swallowed and inhaled on my cigarette. After a short pause, Daniel continued.

"Later on, Mrs. Stetlow started going off on people and swearing at them just like she did to the dogs. If she ran into anyone, she would whisper and hiss, like she was talking to a ghost or something. She thought the neighbors were following her and that everyone was out to get her. She wasn't completely wrong, either. Hardly anyone liked her. No one ever saw her sister, who must have been pretty sick. She never left the house. I think she officially died of cancer, but that wasn't the whole story, which we didn't find out about until later, once they'd taken Mrs. Stetlow away. Apparently, she was so crazy she believed that the neighbors were poisoning their food and making her sister sick. So she stopped feeding her sister. When they came to get her body, it looked like a shriveled-up mummy. I didn't see it, but that's what people said. Maybe they exaggerated, I don't know. But it's true that Mrs. Stetlow kept her sister's body in the house for over two months before anyone realized she was dead. Their next-door neighbor, Mrs. Schneider, finally called the police. She'd been smelling what she thought was their compost pile, but after a while, she realized that something wasn't right. When the police came, Mrs. Stetlow flipped her shit. She threatened them with a knife, ran around screaming. She tried to barricade the doors. The cops had to break the door down, wrestle the knife from her, and take her away. She got put in the psych ward. My mom said that should have happened much sooner. She said that Mrs. Stetlow was clearly clinically paranoid. If people had done something sooner, maybe it wouldn't have turned out so badly."

I stared at Daniel like I was in a trance. "Is she dead?"

"No idea. Maybe. Maybe she's still in the psych ward. That would explain why the house is still empty. Who knows. Maybe the person who inherited it lives in Brazil or somewhere like that. Me and some friends went in a couple of times, although we didn't find any money. At first it was fun and exciting, but whatever. Honestly, I was too creeped out to keep going."

"What is with the basement? There's no floor. There's just gravel everywhere. Sam was sure there was a buried body down there."

"I thought it was weird, too. I asked my dad about it once, you know, hypothetically speaking. He's a real estate agent, and he said gravel basements are not that unusual. In the olden days they used to just leave the foundation like that to save money. A layer of gravel gets the job done."

"What about the unfinished first floor?"

"I don't know about that. Maybe they wanted to renovate it and rent it out, but who knows. You'd have to ask Mrs. Schneider. She knew them better than anyone else. I think she still looks after the place. And you know the weird thing?"

"She has a dog."

"Yep. It's funny because if Mrs. Stetlow knew there was a dog on her property, she would go postal."

"You knew about it the whole time! Why didn't you say anything? You could have tipped me off. I would have told you everything. Eric, Sam, and . . ."—I was about to say Schulz—"I . . . we would've brought you with us. We . . ."

"Dunno." He gave a shrug. "You didn't ask. Anyway, I wasn't paying that much attention."

He gave another shrug.

We were silent for a while. Daniel started a new round in his game. I kept blowing smoke into the thick, silent air of the room. The white noise of the game made me feel calm and kind of spaced out. Finally Daniel stood up, shuffled in his hugely oversized jeans toward the balcony door, and opened it. We sat on the stone floor of the tiny balcony with our bodies squeezed between the wall of the house and the wooden rails. Daniel rolled a joint.

"Eric wouldn't say anything, would he?" I asked. "Don't you think he'll keep quiet?"

"He'd have to be stupid to say anything to the cops about it. Anyway," he paused, lit the joint, inhaled deeply, and blew a long, thick cloud of smoke out of his lungs, "in the end it all just sounds like a crazy story."

"Daniel," I said, looking at him. He cleared his throat and handed me the joint. "Schulz is dead."

"Damn," he answered, and after a few seconds of silence, "Shit."

TWENTY

Through the train window I could see cows grazing. Occasionally a picture-perfect farmhouse would appear and then disappear as the train went past. Only the mountains kept getting bigger the closer I got to them. I was sitting in the smoking section. Across from me was a middle-aged man with a coarse, beer-bloated face. He wore a red-and-white-checkered shirt and would have looked comical if it weren't for the severely angry way the corners of his mouth turned down. I was smoking a cigarette.

The smoke helped cover up the smell of the car: sharp, biting, all-concealing cigarette smoke. I could hold onto that and ward off the self-satisfied body odor of grownups, like some sour combination of salami sandwiches and fabric softener. Smoke smelled the same everywhere, and nothing could withstand it. So I sat on the red-brown pleather bench, watched the landscape fly by, letting myself be hypnotized by it, and smoked. My thoughts oscillated in time to the rumbling of the wheels on the tracks.

Today was Schulz's funeral. I didn't want to go. Maybe that was cowardly, but I couldn't wrap my brain around the event. I didn't want to see Lena, watch her cry, or hear her say again, "He was the only one I really loved." I wouldn't be able to deal with some stupid sermon. I didn't want to see Schulz's parents and his little sister. Maybe they wouldn't say anything to me directly, but they would give me looks that said, "We know you had something to do with his death." I wanted to be left in peace.

I had nothing to do with his death. I would have stopped him from getting in the car if I'd been there. But I wasn't there. I'd slept with his girlfriend, that's all. No one dies from that. And Sam? Sam, I thought, would get out soon. Then everything would go back to how it was before—well, almost. Schulz wasn't coming back. But Sam and Eric. We'd all be back on the skate ramp behind the train tracks soon.

∗ ∙ ∘

I lit another cigarette. Every pretty picture flying past outside was only concealing the darkness lurking behind it. Boredom and desperation were in every street and around every corner, behind every face and in every body. We had only wanted to escape boredom. We had wanted to see things happen. I mean, we weren't even adults.

I'd gone back to the woods and, in the fresh air, dug up the plastic bag. Like a treasure hunter I'd taken seven steps to the right from the duck blind and begun digging at the big tree root. When I found the bag, I took out the letters and burned them in a metal lunch box, which I'd brought along for just that purpose. I took the money and put it in my pocket. My parents were away on vacation; they wouldn't be back for another week. I planned to go to the train station and take a train somewhere: Rome, Paris, Amsterdam, maybe the sea. Anywhere, really, as long as it was away from here.

My plan fell apart before it even began. Waiting in line at the ticket counter at the Munich train station, I realized I probably couldn't rent a hotel room in another city without my parents' signature. I also remembered that I didn't speak Italian or Dutch, and I only knew a few phrases in French. I thought about how school would be starting again soon. I wanted to go. I mean, I actually wanted to go back to school. And so I went to the counter and named the one city that came into my head, since we'd gone there last year on a class trip and it had actually been really cool. I said, "Nuremberg."

"One-way or round-trip?"

I hesitated a minute and wished I'd thought ahead a little bit, but there was a line behind me. I said, "Round-trip, please."

* 6 *

It was early evening when the train arrived at the Nuremberg station. A flurry of activity followed: Suitcases were taken down from the luggage racks, old ladies groaned as they climbed down the steps to the platform, people hobbled and pushed their way down the narrow walkways. I didn't have any luggage. I stuffed my hands into my pockets, pulled the front of my cap down, and sauntered through the train station. I got a hot chocolate at a cafe and people-watched, studying strangers, their faces, and imagining what their stories might be. I watched one young man as he walked past me. His face had a few wrinkles, and he carried a heavy backpack on his shoulders, which made him hunch over slightly as he walked. His face was tan, like he was coming from somewhere in the south. I wanted to ask him where he was coming from, where he'd been staying and for how long, what he experienced there, and what he was going to do next. But I didn't have the guts.

I went to a McDonald's in the station and had a burger, fries, and a Coke. A few yards away I noticed a newspaper stand and thought I'd try reading a magazine or newspaper. I bought a copy of *National Geographic* with a picture of the Mayan pyramids on the cover. They reminded me of Eric and his UFO theories. I grinned, but after reading a few pages, I got bored. It wasn't just the magazine—I was bored with everything. I was alone, and I didn't know what to do with myself. I left the train station and sauntered with my hands in my pockets through the streets of Nuremberg. But I made sure not to wander too far from the station; I didn't want to get lost.

Half a block from the station was a hotel. I slowed down in front of the building and paced back and forth a few times to get my courage up. The front door was glass with a bright, shiny, brass handle. It was heavy; it took some effort to open it. The lobby floor was covered in a plush, apricot-colored carpet, and a man stood behind the dark wood reception desk. He was wearing a black suit with a white shirt.

"Can I help you?" he asked.

I cleared my throat and asked, "How much for a room here?"

"That depends on which one you'd like. We offer a range of options."

He stooped slightly to talk to me, the way you would talk to a child.

"May I ask you, sir, how old you are?"

I raised my head and, out of the dark shadow that my cap cast over my face, looked him straight in the eyes.

"No."

I left the hotel and walked back to the train station. As I was about to go in, a large bundle lying a few yards to the right of the entrance caught my eye. It was a homeless man, his body shrouded in a green parka and his face turned to the wall. I couldn't see anything except the gray-black stubble on his face. He was sleeping.

I reached into my pocket, pulled out all the money I had left, thirty-eight hundred marks, and put it into the pocket of his parka. Then I went home.